D0823263

AFTER THE CRASH

AFTER THE CRASH

HOW TO GUARD YOUR MONEY IN THESE TURBULENT TIMES

GARTH TURNER

KEY PORTER BOOKS

Copyright © 2009 by Garth Turner

All rights reserved. No part of this work covered by the copyrights hereon may be repro-
duced or used in any form or by any means—graphic, electronic or mechanical, including
photocopying, recording, taping or information storage and retrieval systems—without
the prior written permission of the publisher, or, in case of photocopying or other repro-
graphic copying, a licence from Access Copyright, the Canadian Copyright Licensing
Agency, One Yonge Street, Suite 1900, Toronto, Ontario, M6B 3A9.

Library and Archives Canada Cataloguing in Publication

Turner, Garth
    After the crash : how to guard your money in these turbulent times / Garth Turner.

ISBN 978-1-55470-182-7

    1. Finance, Personal--Canada. 2. Financial security. 3. Investments.
I. Title.

HG179.T863 2009   332.024'010971   C2008-907523-4

ONTARIO ARTS COUNCIL
CONSEIL DES ARTS DE L'ONTARIO

The publisher gratefully acknowledges the support of the Canada Council for the Arts
and the Ontario Arts Council for its publishing program. We acknowledge the support of
the Government of Ontario through the Ontario Media Development Corporation's
Ontario Book Initiative.

We acknowledge the financial support of the Government of Canada through the Book
Publishing Industry Development Program (BPIDP) for our publishing activities.

Key Porter Books Limited
Six Adelaide Street East, Tenth Floor
Toronto, Ontario
Canada M5C 1H6

www.keyporter.com

Electronic formatting: Alison Carr

Printed and bound in Canada

09 10 11 12 5 4 3 2 1

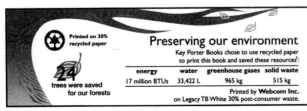

Preserving our environment

Key Porter Books chose to use recycled paper
to print this book and saved these resources[1]:

	energy	water	greenhouse gases	solid waste
	17 million BTUs	33,422 L	965 kg	515 kg

Printed on 30%
recycled paper

24 trees were saved
for our forests

Printed by **Webcom Inc.**
on Legacy TB White 30% post-consumer waste.

FSC

Mixed Sources

Product group from well-managed
forests, and recycled wood or fiber

Cert no. SW-COC-002358
www.fsc.org
© 1996 Forest Stewardship Council

[1]Estimates were made using the Environmental Defense Paper Calculator.

CONTENTS

BEFORE WE BEGIN . . .

The crash happened in the autumn of 2008. After the crash is now. This book is about what comes next, and what you should do about it. Immediately.

While every generation screws up its finances, makes bad decisions and pays the price, there's a sense that we really did a number this time. Real estate obsession ended up whacking the middle class and has led to the greatest economic crisis since the 1930s. Too much borrowing, spending, and speculation, together with rampant cowboy capitalism, has hobbled America and its transformational president. Canadians may think they're just collateral damage, but we're right in the thick of this mess.

In the summer of 2006, it became apparent we were headed for a cliff. The way had just been cleared for young couples to buy houses in Canada without money. Added to no-money down payments were new 40-year mortgages which increased both debt and house prices. Within a year, half of all new home loans would be for terms longer than 25 years. The price of an average home in Toronto, Calgary, or Vancouver was between five and nine times the average family income. The savings rate was zero. The stock market was soaring. Alberta was booming and so were SUV sales. In my community outside of Toronto the country's biggest home-builder was turning out new houses—one a day—from an assembly line in a giant building in a former farm field and selling them to couples who could finance them on a credit card. The government was cutting taxes. Banks had stopped doing appraisals and were approving mortgages based on postal codes. Within a few months, the price of a home reached $771,000 in Vancouver, $505,000 in Calgary, and $399,000 in Toronto. The government said the economy was "as solid as the Canadian Shield." Taxes were cut again. People lined up in the snow to buy new condos which, as it turned out, would never be built.

Meanwhile in the US, the greatest financial bubble in history was deflating. Home prices collapsed, first in California and Florida, then almost everywhere. Middle-class families were shocked to see their net worth erased so fast, and immediately cut back on consumer spending, skidding car sales and halting construction. The first reports started spreading about how billions in loans on all those devalued properties had been sold by major Wall Street banks—global institutions that would not exist any more in two years. That summer I warned that Canada's real estate market, and then its economy, would trace the unhappy path of our southern neighbour.

In early 2008, *Greater Fool: The Troubled Future of Real Estate*, was published, in which I forecast an immediate real estate bust and coming financial woes. Academics and industry experts discounted it. Six months later, we were all in crisis.

It's hard to diminish this. The stock market lost half its value in a few weeks. Wall Street banks collapsed. The auto industry crumbled. Washington had to bail out the biggest insurer, the biggest bank, and the biggest mortgage companies. Millions of people lost their homes. Millions lost their jobs. Ottawa and Washington sank into deficit as they poured billions into bailing out bankers. Just months after telling homeowners, investors, and workers everything was cool, politicians told us this could be the prelude to another depression.

So here we are, after the crash, but in a prelude to what?

- How safe are the big Canadian banks? Could the stock market lose 90 percent of its value, as happened 80 years ago? Will house prices fall by half, meaning millions of families owe more on their mortgages than their homes are worth?
- Could a bad recession spin into a depression?
- Should you convert savings into gold, just in case?
- Are families who are buying generators and taking cash out of the bank just kooks, or are they smart?
- What happens in a long, painful time of deflation?

Hardly a day goes by now that the notion of depression is not in the media, despite the frantic and expensive attempts by government to prevent it. Yes, nobody alive under the age of 90 has experienced a time when the economy collapses and stays there for years. Today's problems started with a real estate bubble bursting, which was quickly replaced by a banking and financial crisis, then became an epidemic of unemployment. So, it's far more serious. But what now?

THE NEW FACE OF DEPRESSION?

Some people think a new depression's inevitable, and it would look like this:

Suburbs devalue and depopulate, leaving a checkerboard of abandoned homes where the weeds grow and weathered For Sale signs wave in the wind. Crime everywhere is more of a problem, as municipal budgets plunge and police services are strained. Transit systems no longer operate every day. The highways leading downtown are no longer clogged. Towns and small cities which depended on a now-shuttered Chrysler supplier plant or a forest products mill are quiet, with empty Main Streets and abandoned Best Buy and Home Depot stores. Just the Walmart remains, its parking lot always busy. People eat at home most of the time now, and almost everyone who can, has a garden.

Major highways have been turned into toll roads and after a

big storm, it now takes weeks for the electrical grid to be restored. Financial institutions no longer allow online banking after a web-based run on deposits, and have imposed daily withdrawal limits. Baby Boomers once yearning for retirement now realize they're never going to sell their big homes, and shut off rooms to conserve heat. University enrolments, now unaffordable to most families, plunge. Once again, three generations share a home. RRSPs based on stocks and mutual funds have pretty much hit zero.

Far-fetched?

Hard to say, since the only modern industrialized country to have gone through a protracted economic crisis since the Great Crash of 1929 is Japan. It, too, had a real estate bubble which turned average homes unaffordable for average families. Its banks, like ours, were heavily involved in leverage and speculation. Its stock market, like the Dow and TSX, hit historic highs just as home prices also peaked. And like us, it crashed.

Unlike us, however, Japanese families saved more than 15 percent of their incomes, while we saved nothing. Unlike us, the Japanese bubble built for five years while ours built for three times as long, and was three times larger relative to the economy. Unlike us, the Japanese did not borrow against home equity to finance consumer spending, and unlike the crash in America, the Japanese mess did not involve bundling together worthless mortgages and selling them across the globe, infecting country after country.

Yes, despite those factors making Japan's descent less precipitous than ours, the ride has been rough. And long. Years and years long. As Marcus Gee reported in *The Globe and Mail* in late 2008:

> When the bubble finally burst, it was a wipeout. The Nikkei dropped by two-thirds over the next two years. Commercial land values in the big cities fell by 80 percent between 1991 and 2000. They never returned to bubble levels. Neither did stocks. Today the Nikkei stands at one-fifth

of its 1989 peak. If the Toronto stock exchange were to perform as badly, the index would stand at 3,000 in 2027...

Home values are 40 percent lower than they were when the bubble burst, and total public debt has grown to 180 percent of the economy, the highest of any industrialized country, and a guarantee that Japanese babies born today will be paying far higher taxes than their parents.

There is no accurate model for financial and economic meltdown. Governments in Ottawa, Washington, London, Paris, Beijing, Moscow, and Madrid have been desperate in their actions to prevent global collapse, dropping interest rates, nationalizing teetering banks, and spending staggering amounts. This is exactly what Tokyo did and yet, even with interest rates at zero and massive bailouts, life turned tough and stayed there.

With luck, it will be different this time. Hopefully the post-bubble years will bring merely a bad recession we snap out of by 2011 or 2012. But there's no guarantee. At the least, Canadians should get used to the idea their houses and investments will be worth far less, jobs will be harder to find, and our standard of living will dive. At the worst, well, we could relive experiences which have been all but forgotten here—difficult days complicated by an age in which gas stations and grocery stores don't function offline, and most people don't carry cash. Without this modern, enveloping, and functioning infrastructure, what would happen? Even over the course of a few months, or weeks? What would you do?

This book won't tell you precisely what happens over the coming years, since that is unknown. However, it gives a range of options and possible scenarios—together with a suite of actions and strategies you and your family can take to defend your money, and hopefully prosper. After you read the factors which got us here, and the trends now propelling current events, the ultimate decision is yours on how aggressively you prepare, or how much you pray you don't have to.

CHAPTER ONE

STRUCTURED BY COWS

"Without a garden in that back yard," she said, "we would not have survived."

The yard was in eastside Vancouver. The years were 1929 through 1934. The woman was now ninety, and the time was October of 2008. "There are some lessons," she said, "we've been wrong to forget."

About the time she spoke those words, recalling how her husband lost his job as a cop after being whacked on the head in a labour scuffle, her old house was on the market for $949,000. There was a new kitchen and a hot tub on the back deck, covering the soil that once saved a family, but it was still a cramped 1,200 square feet. "Fix me up!" the listing agent had written under the picture on MLS.ca.

"We bought that house for $850. Thank God we finally paid it off," she said. "And that it had a yard."

In the late spring of 2008, Mark the local electrician was finishing installing the generator at my cottage on Lake Erie. We'd settled on a Wallenstein model kicking out 7,200 watts from a 13-horsepower Honda gas engine with an electric start Dorothy could easily operate. Mark got an area guy to build a shed for it and without my asking, they anchored it on six-by-six posts sunk four feet into the earth, and then installed lateral beams between the feet and poured in cement. Above, they installed three locks, then deformed the inside bolts so they might never be removed.

Mark buried the transfer cable deep. Inside the cottage he connected it to a new panel of breakers, separating circuits for the generator and the electrical grid. He added a voltmeter to monitor the flow of each, and a box of lights to show when power was coming from the outside world.

When I got there on a Friday afternoon he was leaning on the hood of his white van, writing up the invoice.

"Why," I asked, "did you do all that?"

Surprised, he said, "So they can't take it. What'd you think?" I thought that was extreme.

Then Mark told me about his generator business. Actually, it was a sideline for a guy who wires barns and industrial units, but lately it had overwhelmed him. "I even sent my boy, Paul, to Wisconsin," he said, "to take the factory course. Glad that happened."

Every single sale—and there were scores of them—of a residential, natural gas-powered generator located in a nearby city, he added, had come from word of mouth. "And I can't keep up."

Two months later, Paul installed a 13-kilowatt, 426-pound unit behind a privacy fence beside my urban home. He showed me how it powered automatically when the grid goes brown, then black.

"And if you saw what we do," he laughed, "you'd know what's coming."

When 2008 started, five major investment banks controlled Wall Street; 50 percent of all the mortgages in the US were owed to two publicly traded companies; the Dow was at 13,500; and oil was on its way to $140 a barrel. When the year ended, three of those banks were gone, the mortgage companies had been nationalized, the stock market had lost 40 percent of its value, and oil had collapsed by half.

GM and Chrysler were merging. Governments around the world were taking over banks and rushing to guarantee deposits. Twelve million American families owed more on their mortgages than their homes were worth. Four million more were behind on their payments. Condo towers in downtown Toronto, Calgary, and Vancouver were gaping holes in the ground surrounded by chain-link fence, collecting rain water. In Iceland, the government took over the major banks, the stock market fell 76 percent, and then interest rates jumped 6 percent in a day. Stock markets in New York and Toronto saw their greatest one-day losses on record. Days later, their greatest gains.

As stock markets gyrated wildly, a Conference Board survey showed consumer confidence in the US at the lowest point in 40 years. More seriously, it indicated that most people believed things would get far worse before they improved—a virtual guarantee of slumping car sales, idled assembly plants in Ontario and Ohio, and rising unemployment. In just 12 months, the Canadian economy had lost 200,000 jobs and the US more than 760,000 jobs. But by the end of 2008, losses in America were closer to 200,000 a month. Companies were asking Ottawa if they could stop making pension payments to retired workers. Lobbyists for the auto parts and forestry sectors were begging for bailouts as northern mill towns and southern factories turned out the lights.

Suddenly a consumer-led recession, based initially on a devastating housing slump, was transforming into something more troubling: a jobless depression. Meanwhile, real estate spiraled lower. In suburban Toronto, the region's biggest homebuilder slashed prices by $50,000 and still watched business collapse. In London, Ontario, new homebuyers picked up keys to a free new car with their cheaper new house. In Kelowna, homeowners watched as equity in the average home drained away at the rate of $11,000 a month.

But events to the south in late 2008 and early 2009 showed Canadians that the worst was likely still to come:

- In Monterey County, California, the average home price dropped to $280,000, a 65 percent decline from the average of $799,500 a year earlier.
- Home prices in twenty cities fell almost 17 percent year-over-year, with declines of 31 percent in Phoenix and Las Vegas and more than 25 percent in Los Angeles, Miami, San Diego, and San Francisco.
- Half of all homeowners in Nevada with a mortgage owed more to the banks than their homes were worth.
- By the time the housing market bottoms, prices will have collapsed by 40 percent and four in ten homeowners will have negative equity, said New York University economics professor Nouriel Roubini.
- Ground zero: the great, sprawling suburbs surrounding cities like Chicago, Toronto, San Francisco, and Calgary, where armies of homeowners bought near-identical houses from builders, with little or nothing down. After all, with values falling and energy costs rising, with commuting costs going up and job prospects fading, who'd want to live in the middle of a former field, where it takes a litre of gas to go and fetch a litre of milk?

"We are headed for a depression," Euro-Pacific Capital president Peter Schiff said in a late 2008 interview with the *Financial Post*. "Whatever we call it, we're still going to be in it at the end of Obama's term. He's going to be known as a depression-era president."

That week, a woman name Lana posted this on my blog: "I just turned 61. My husband is 63. He almost had a job at Home Depot, but I think it was his age that kept him from getting one. He hates Walmart, but what choice does he have? He has to work. Thirty-two years at the same place, and it was 'Goodbye Charlie'…to over 20 people over 60 in one day.

"Yeah, we are tightening our belts. Growing and canning our own food where we can. Eating lots of leftovers."

The same day, Mobil-Exxon announced profits of $14 billion thanks to the short-lived commodity price bubble, and American Express laid off 7,000 employees, thanks to the fact some of the most creditworthy and wealthy Americans could no longer pay their bills.

Within days came word that major American banks, each losing as much as $1 billion a month on credit card losses, had banded together to forgive some consumer debt. In a desperate bid to retrieve at least some of the $900 billion that shoppers had rung up on plastic, the banks launched a program to waive up to 40 percent of the money owed them, letting cardholders pay the rest back over time.

"Credit cards," said an Associated Press report, "the ubiquitous plastic rectangles that have become an integral part of American life and the economy, now look to be the latest domino to drop in a financial crisis that started with subprime mortgages and continually takes new twists."

Mortgages and credit cards at the heart of a global financial crisis. Could it get any worse?

Writing in the *New York Times* that week about the 1930s, economist Gregory Mankiw said, "even if another Depression were around the corner, you shouldn't expect much advance warning from the economics profession."

Could that mean we're already there? If so, what will you do?

In an excessive ballroom in the excessive Gaylord Opryland Convention Centre in Nashville, I stood in front of 1,600 realtors from across America to tell them what the future might hold. Foreclosures were at that moment running 71 percent ahead of year-ago statistics and the average price of housing had taken its biggest drop ever on the S&P/Case-Shiller House Price Index.

An hour earlier I was walking past the Grand Ole Opry on my way to the gig, when a couple asked me to take their picture. I noticed the Harley T-shirts, and asked if they rode. Absolutely, they said, from Texas, sir. And the bike was pretty much all they had since losing the house.

I told the realtors how much the meltdown felt like the aftermath of 9/11, with crashing interest rates and risky financial markets, instability and yet opportunity. They gave me a standing ovation for not scaring the crap out of them, and I flew back to Toronto where I did an odd thing. I cashed in the cheque for my speaking fee. Cash, all in twenties.

Dorothy just stared at me funny when I got back in the car. So I told her about the garden.

Seldom in the past 70 years has there been this much financial stress. Too few of us understand how it all happened. Worse, it's totally unclear what comes next. In the absence of this information, families, investors, and homeowners can hardly be expected to know what course of action to follow to protect themselves, or seek shelter.

Sure, cash money, generators, and gardens are one option. But so is doing nothing and waiting for the storm to blow over. After all, lousy times have come and gone before, recessions have cost jobs and homes, and we've survived. So, why is this one any different?

Without a doubt, a majority of people are doing just that. Some are so caught up in the suburban-big-box-minivan-kids lifestyle that crashing stock indices and currency fluctuations go largely unnoticed. They'll stay unaware until financial reality invades their lives, maybe as a declined credit card, a called line of credit, a job loss, or listing the family home for vastly less than it was supposed to be worth.

Then, like everyone else, they'll have a "where-the-hell-did-this-come-from" moment, months after Lehman Brothers employees were cleaning out their desks or Suncor execs in Calgary were pulling the plug on a new oil sands upgrader. That's the thing about this financial meltdown—it's real, pervasive, and spreads like the Spanish flu. You can feel fine in the morning, and be gasping for air by sunset. It infects families through so many entry points, like germs on the car door, brought into the home through a higher mortgage payment, a car lease that ends in obscene charges, a missed promotion or lost pay hike, a gutted RRSP statement, a new home suddenly worth less than what you owe on it, or a retirement torn apart by greedy investors in some other country.

Other people just deny it all. Like realtors. Like my friend who's the spokesguy for a major national real estate marketing company. His words are written down by reporters and then fed to first-time homebuyers as the trusted thoughts of an "expert." Like politicians who tell voters everything's under control, such folks try to manipulate information in order to get the result they want. In this case, anything but a disaster.

In a Toronto hotel packed with housing industry players, my friend gave a speech recently in which he said: "Looking forward, we anticipate a continuation of stable market activity, minus the urgency present in past. Gone are the multiple offers that left both buyers and sellers dissatisfied. The increase in the number of homes listed for sale is a definite advantage for purchasers who now have the luxury of time in making one of the most important decisions of a lifetime. For sellers, the time to trade up has never been better.

"Canadians are great believers in homeownership—a fact underscored by the close to 70 percent who own homes in this country. History has proven time and time again that real estate is a solid, long-term investment that appreciates at a rate of about five percent annually. You can't live in your mutual fund, and after the last month in the financial markets, quite frankly, we're not sure you'd want to."

Soothing. But are they weasel words?

About the same time, Laurie Campbell, executive director of Credit Canada, which provides credit counselling for consumers, was pointing out that Canadians have basically no savings, maxed-out credit cards, more mortgage debt than ever before, and live in an economy rapidly losing altitude. According to CIBC World Markets, consumer credit accounts for 40 percent of personal disposable income, while mortgage debt accounts for 90.6 percent of disposable income.

The conclusion, says Campbell: "It's one of the worst times to be in debt. You're done, you're screwed."

Screwed or not, there are always things people can do, actions families can take, moves investors can make, to soften the blow, avoid losses and survive. That's the intent of this book. We'll go through a three-step process. First, let's understand how the world came unraveled so completely and quickly.

Was this the fault of lower-income Americans who wanted to move from trailer parks to McMansions, and the mortgage brokers who spotted them the money in Ninja loans (no income, no job, no assets)? Does anyone actually still believe that? Or are we to blame the greedy, unprincipled, Porsche-driving investment bankers on Wall Street who packaged all those toxic mortgages into securities they then sold to unsuspecting investors around the world? Or the rating agencies who slapped AAA labels on crap assets? (In testimony before a Congressional committee this email from a Standard and Poor's employee came to light: "We rate every deal. It could be structured by cows and we would rate it." Responded committee chairman Henry Waxman: "The story of the credit rating agencies is a story of colossal failure. The result is that our entire financial system is now at risk." On the Internet, dozens of "Structured by Cows" websites sprang up overnight.)

Or did the blame belong to regulators and politicians who turned a blind eye while times were good, allowed a shadow banking system to develop in which credit swaps and derivatives became the world's biggest-ever Ponzi scheme? Or those policy makers whose actions helped twist a healthy, robust housing market in which everyone grew more prosperous into a bubble destined to burst? Who was it who dreamed up subprime mortgages in the States, or zero-down payments and 40-year amortizations in Canada? Did they even consider the consequences? Or did everyone actually think real estate—like the stock market—could go up forever, juiced on borrowed money? When the average home price in Vancouver hit $771,321 in March of 2008, did anyone seriously think it could last? ("Residential sales continue to be strong, but there is a lot more choice on the market today. This is good news for a market that has been defined by record-breaking activity for most of this decade," said Real Estate Board of Greater Vancouver president Dave Watt that month.)

How about the central bankers and other smart guys running the monetary system of North America? After all, Fed chairman Alan Greenspan was at the helm after 9/11, and engineered the interest rate collapse which made money too cheap not to borrow, helping inflate that post-terrorist, patriot-fuelling real estate bubble. His successor, Ben Bernanke, drank from the same cup after the collapse of 2008, dropping the overnight bank rate down to just 1 percent.

As *MarketWatch* editor-in-chief David Galloway said then, "But Bernanke is quickly running out of monetary bullets, with the risk of having to take the extraordinary step of someday lowering interest rates to zero just a bank run or two away right now. Japan, which spent five unproductive years at zero between 2001 and 2006 before boosting to a half percentage point, is now talking about a quarter point cut and possibly a return to zero, even though it didn't work last time." As Galloway rightly notes, when the cost of borrowing hits nothing, then so does the return on savings and, "How's that for an invitation to go out and spend?"

In Canada, Bank of Canada governor Mark Carney, himself a 13-year veteran of Wall Street while working at Goldman Sachs, followed suit, chopping the bank rate to just over 2 percent, half of what it had been a year earlier. In a news conference when the American stock market was at a low unseen since 1931, Carney said, "The sky is not falling, the sky is still there. We do not have the imbalances in our economy that other economies have going into this time of difficulty."

More weasel words? After all, tens of billions of dollars had just been carved out of pension plans and RRSPs belonging to average folks, many of whom would never live long enough to make it back and didn't have a public service pension. It sounded like Carney might have been right at home wearing a fedora.

Second, we better figure out what lies ahead. That determines everything else.

Time to flee the suburbs for the hills, where you can at least have chickens? Or are these the days to be bottom-feeding for distressed real estate and loading up on that cheap borrowed money?

The answer will come from wherever it is that we land in a few years. Politicians, bankers, and realtors are hoping and praying this is a mild recession, shallow and short. A more realistic view is that we're in for a year, maybe three, of tough sledding, with rising unemployment, collapsing car sales, stagnant real estate, declining prices, and a recession which lasts until at least 2010 with no recovery in family finances until 2012 or so.

But it could be a lot worse. A disaster, actually—a new version of the Dirty Thirties, but with high-speed Internet and iPods, in which personal wealth is destroyed, especially that wealth which was built on a foundation of personal debt. Like real estate. In this scenario, housing in every major market in Canada loses up to half its value. Recent buyers, especially young couples who put little down, are trapped in money-sucking homes soon worth less than their mortgage, and which they can't afford to sell.

After all, a suburban home bought for $400,000 in early 2008 for 5 percent down could be worth (if you're lucky, and can find a buyer) $350,000 at the end of 2009. That's a loss of $50,000, plus a sales commission of $17,000 or so, which means the hapless vendors would have to show up on closing day with a cheque for at least $50,000 ($30,000 for the mortgage shortfall, plus closing costs) just to get out. The question then: Why bother, when personal bankruptcy might well be preferable to having no house and yet a new $50,000 debt? The next question: How many of the tens of thousands of recent buyers would follow suit? And what would the impact be on the values of every nearly identical property in all those 'burbs?

This is a nightmare scenario which has already gripped the American middle class. It destroys the very asset at the heart of family wealth. It leads to an economic collapse governments have so far tried to stem with interest rate extremism and trillions in taxpayer-funded bailouts. Best efforts aside, we may be but a few months away from this reality.

In fact, how could we not be? As I argued in the early 2008 book, *Greater Fool*, there's no valid argument—realtors and central bankers aside—to counter the stark similarity of the American and Canadian experiences. We both fell in love with real estate. We inflated values beyond sustainable levels. We both lowered the bar for mortgage financing. We turned a boom into a bubble. We both overbuilt, overpriced, overbought, and over-mortgaged. And then it all blew up.

As Merrill Lynch Canada economist David Wolf has pointed out, there's but one key difference between the experiences of the two countries: Canada is almost exactly two years behind. "What worries us is that Canadian households have been running a larger financial deficit than households in either the US or the UK," Wolf wrote in his late 2008 report. "Canada's housing market seems to be tracking the US. Why the two-year lag? It may be because the Canadian market had more room to run, having remained weaker for longer than the US market through the 1990s. It may be because the commodity price boom had kept national income and thus consumer fundamentals stronger in Canada over the past couple of years. It may be because Canadian lending standards were slower to loosen."

Whatever, Wolf told reporters, he's getting, "more alarmed by the day."

So, guess what's coming?

I've already given you some statistics on the mess Americans have made of their real estate market, and they'll be repeated here in Canada, in large part. Valuations will plunge, transactions will be further curtailed, and many people will wonder why the hell they ever agreed to take on gargantuan mortgages. As more factories close and industries consolidate, jobs will be lost and real estate values in some areas pushed far lower than the norm. The spring market—traditionally the best of the year—just won't exist in 2009, or maybe even 2010. Or beyond.

Hardest hit will be single-industry communities where mills and plants wither and die. That's easy to see. But also mauled will be regions, like southern Ontario, which have built a heavy dependence on the car business. As GM and Chrysler merge, for example, you can count on at least one of the giant assembly plants—in Brampton or Oshawa—shuttering for good.

In Alberta, volatile and unpredictable oil prices and a global recession have already exacted a toll. Some key expansion plans for the oil sands in the North have been shelved by energy giants, while further south homeowners have seen equity vanish. By late 2008, the average house price in Edmonton was down $64,000, or 17 percent from the peak, while in Calgary the loss was $62,000, or almost 14 percent.

In Toronto, with more than 34,000 condo units in the pipeline and a credit freeze spreading, the scene is set for a crash in the value of high-rise units which will ripple north from the downtown towers. As in Vancouver, high-profile developments where scores of units have already been sold to speculators and dewy-eyed young couples, will simply never be built. Average prices in the Toronto core by the beginning of 2009 were down 15 percent from the peak, and sales were lower by 21 percent from the same period a year earlier.

On the West coast, despite the 2010 Olympic Games, a real estate disaster is brewing. Hardest hit will be recent condo buyers, who shelled out $300,000 for a unit just big enough to park my motorcycles in. During the first nine months of 2007, the city of Vancouver issued building permits for 3,842 residential units. In the same period in 2008, that withered to 1,476. The Real Estate Board reported September sales were down 43 percent from the previous year, while listings grew by 29 percent. The next month, way worse: sales off 55 percent; listings up 76 percent.

"I've never seen anything so deep, so fast," said Eric Carlson, the CEO of Anthem Properties Corp. told the local daily "I used to be a know-it-all. Now, I'm pretty humble."

Humble now. Scared comes later, because if Canada repeats the US experience (and I'm telling you it will), not only will hundreds of millions of dollars worth of developments be abandoned, but billions of dollars of existing real estate will be affected. A city where almost 100 percent of household net worth is in housing, where families struggle with the greatest mortgage burden in the country and where more than 70 percent of personal disposal income is required just to own the average home, is a city at risk.

But this will not merely be a collapse in real estate values across our nation, but also a repudiation of the cult of housing. The effects will be profound, as a home is seen no longer as a risk-less investment that always appreciates in value, and as our addiction to sprawling suburbanity is suddenly viewed harshly, through new eyes.

"Strange days are upon the residents of many a suburban cul-de-sac," begins an article by Christopher Leinberger published in 2008 in the *Atlantic Monthly*, titled "The next slum?"

"Once-tidy yards have become overgrown, as the houses they front have gone vacant. Signs of physical and social disorder are spreading. " The piece goes on to describe how middle class values don't stand a chance—in the 'burbs or anywhere else—when middle class finances fade:

> At Windy Ridge, a recently built starter-home development seven miles northwest of Charlotte, North Carolina, 81 of the community's 132 small, vinyl-sided houses were in foreclosure as of late last year. Vandals have kicked in doors and stripped the copper wire from vacant houses; drug users and homeless people have furtively moved in. In December, after a stray bullet blasted through her son's bedroom and into her own, Laurie Talbot, who'd moved to Windy Ridge from New York in 2005, told *The Charlotte Observer*, "I thought I'd bought a home in Pleasantville. I never imagined in my wildest dreams that stuff like this would happen."
>
> In the Franklin Reserve neighborhood of Elk Grove, California, south of Sacramento, the houses are nicer than those at Windy Ridge—many once sold for well over $500,000—but the phenomenon is the same. At the height of the boom, 10,000 new homes were built there in just four years. Now many are empty; renters of dubious character occupy others. Graffiti, broken windows, and other markers of decay have multiplied. Susan McDonald, president of the local residents' association and an executive at a local bank, told the Associated Press, "There's been gang activity. Things have really been changing, the last few years."

In Canada's Parliament, for a while, I represented people living in an endless tract of suburbs.

They call them the Xburbs—the urban sprawl that radiates for 100 kilometers in every direction from downtown Toronto. This is where the GenXers went to buy McMansions built on an assembly line by Mattamy Homes and then planted on Class A farmland. They did this because they could get 3,000 square feet of new house with granite countertops, stainless appliances, media rooms, double car garages, and a better lifestyle than their parents achieved after fifty years, instantly. Often the down payment was next to nothing, just 1.5 percent of purchase price. And with a 40-year mortgage, monthly payments were lessened. It meant a quality of life could be had without the bother of a lifetime of work. What's not to like?

Fifty years ago suburbs offered a release from the grime and proximity of urban living. They gave what only rich people could afford then—space, the illusion of nature, convenience, and modernity. They were also important because of homogeneity. The suburbs were quintessentially middle-class and upwardly mobile, with decent schools and an utter sameness which was comforting after the unevenness of city life and the War.

Like you, perhaps, I was a child of this lifestyle. Cars, lawns, predictable neighbours, dogs, curvy streets, shopping centres, and more suburbs, all connected with arterial roads and controlled-access highways which eventually snaked away to a pointy downtown. For decades, this was a choice place to aspire to. But with what is now happening, we question the very premise of the 'burbs.

Futurist James Howard Kunstler has called them the greatest waste of infrastructure in human history, and he's right. After all, the 'burbs only work when there are cars, and the energy needed to make them run has become precious. Second, the urban sprawl which the suburbs by definition create has given society a problem akin to that faced by the Roman Empire—millions of people now live far from services and supplies, and bringing those lines closer is bankrupting everyone. Third, the suburbs, populated with wasteful single-family homes left empty too often and only partially occupied the rest of the time, sitting on land which once produced crops, sucking endless energy and water through miles of pipes and tubes, where residents trade gas for milk in a distant, centralized shopping area to avoid lower property values through neighbourhood commercialization, are an environmental nightmare. Fourth, demographics and the growing need for Boomers to convert homes into cash dooms the kind of homes most of them now own. Fifth, suburbs are about to suffer the greatest blow—falling out of fashion—killed off by the financial crisis of 2009 and beyond.

This leads us to the future. What'll happen to the suburbs? Especially now?

Clearly, their time is ending. Suburbs need cars, and our car-centric culture is threatened as never before. Until alternatives to the oil-fuelled internal combustion engine are reliable and afford-able, the 'burbs will decline in popularity. The energy crisis also underscores the massive mistakes policy makers have left us with—miles of houses without stores, streetscapes nobody wants to walk down, infrastructure so inefficient that property taxes become unaffordable, whole new populated landscapes without shade trees or moderating open waters and where per-unit energy consumption is unparalleled. Worse, we have mass-produced homes of building materials with a life expectancy measured in decades, not centuries.

But while the long trend is for buyers to fall out of love with the suburbs, financial contagion is the immediate threat. And how could it not be? We practically imported it.

While the US housing market was being puffed up, then destroyed, by subprime mortgages which allowed people with little money to buy big houses, Canadian media looked south-ward in clucking disapproval. All the while, of course, our regulators were doing the same thing—with consequences which will be most evident in the sprawling 'burbs.

Caving to demands from the mortgage business in its first budget, the new Conservative government in 2006 liberalized lending rules. Soon after, the Canada Mortgage and Housing Corporation said it would be making home ownership "more affordable and accessible to Canadians" by doing some extraordi-nary and very "un-Canadian" things.

Like allowing interest-only mortgage payments for up to the first 10 years on the purchase or refinance of a home.

"This new option will give borrowers greater flexibility in managing their cash flow," said the federal agency. But, of course, this had the effect of turning mortgages into rent, since interest-only payments did not build up a dollar in equity. But it was a perfect move for a bubble market—allowing investors to carry a property at minimal cost while rising prices created a tax-free capital gain. The argument that this made speculation, not home-owning, easier was tough to refute.

But that was just the start of the Canadian subprime movement or, as was aptly described in America, "the race for the bottom."

Canada also moved to extend the payback period for mortgages, from the traditional 25 years to 35 years and, finally, to 40. The result was lower monthly mortgage charges and, more importantly, the ability of people to buy more "house" with the same income. Royal Bank economists, for example, calculated that someone able to afford a $302,000 bungalow with a 25-year amortization could suddenly afford a house costing $343,000 simply by goosing the amortization by 15 years. So, without buyers getting any wealthier, the value of houses could rise by 13 percent. So, they did.

The downside, of course, was more debt—in two ways. First, longer payback periods let people carry more debt, just like those low-introductory-rate subprimes that had suckered consumers into King Kong-sized borrowings in the States. Second, bigger amortizations meant far more mortgage interest would accumulate over the years. For example, a $300,000 loan at 7 percent paid back over 25 years would cost a total of $630,373. But drag out the repayment period by 15 years, and that bill mushroomed to almost $885,000.

So long as the bubble lasted, though, and house values escalated wildly, who cared? Obviously not a majority of buyers, as 40-year amortizations captured a stunning 37 percent of the market within a year and an estimated 60 percent in the second. Consumers weren't dumb. In a rising market, why struggle to pay anything off?

But there was more bubble-puffing to come, courtesy of Ottawa. In addition to no-repayment loans and 40-year mortgages came the government's blessing to buy a house without any actual money. It was the ultimate subprime move. CMHC endorsed a 100 percent financing program requiring no down payment, which meant lenders giving buyers all that debt would now be covered by government insurance. To qualify, homebuyers simply had to be in debt already (with a credit card or a bank loan) and have a job. Oh yes, and even the mortgage insurance premium buyers were required to pay could be wrapped into the mortgage debt itself.

But there was still more. Clever lenders started allowing consumers to put closing costs, including land transfer taxes and legal bills, on to their loan amount. Suddenly mortgages were approved for 103 percent of the value of a home. Canadians who had snickered at the insanity of Ditech.com commercials, broadcast on American TV, offering home loans for more than a home was worth, had suddenly crossed to the other side.

The bubblification of the country was complete:

- No-interest loans.
- Repayment over four decades.
- Bigger mortgages on the same income.
- Zero down payment.
- Mortgages for more than the cost of the house
- All government approved, at no risk to the lender, thanks to insurance from Ottawa.

And we got the results you'd expect from letting people without money buy houses. Mortgage debt increased by $100 billion in a year to almost $900 billion by late 2008, and what had been a strong housing market in 2006 turned into a speculative, out-of-control frothy excess destined for misery.

Especially in Sprawlville.

Every 24 hours the big metal door rolls up and another house emerges from a windowless white building the size of a football field sitting in a former farmer's field outside of Milton, Ontario. This has been the fastest-growing community in Canada, where municipal councilors burst with pride in 2007 as the place swelled at the obscene annual rate of 72 percent.

And while the locals complain that the eight-minute, cross-town trip of a few years ago can now take half an hour in snarled, bumper-to-bumper traffic, thousands of new residents have poured in every year, refugees from the even-worse mess of neighbouring Mississauga and the concrete urbanity of Toronto, 45 minutes down the 401 (twice that in rush hour).

Like many development hot spots, but probably more so, Milton happily crawled into the deep pocket of a real estate developer, Mattamy Homes. The tryst has paid off for each. Milton has been loaned millions to convert sleepy roads into arterial flyways, has exploded its tax base, and has even been given endless acres for a new university campus. Mattamy, in return, hardly seems to pause for zoning changes and development permits while it chews through land, turning vistas at the base of the Niagara Escarpment into seas of new homes.

So confident was Mattamy of selling out a new 1,000-house subdivision on the spreading western flank of the town that it built the country's largest house factory, where robots tirelessly hammer nails into studs and workers install shingles on roofs sitting on the concrete floor. After passing through ten work stations, finished homes—chandeliers hung, tiles grouted, floors shined, and toilets plumbed—emerge at the rate of one a day, are hoisted on a giant modified flatbed, and trucked to a waiting foundation.

What Henry Ford was to cars, Mattamy is to houses. And after a factory home is plunked on a pre-poured base, even before there is landscaping or grass or a driveway; while backhoes and dump trucks still grind by, kicking up a choking layer of dust that cakes minivans, front porches, and pets, the families move in. After all, they must. They're on a financial knife's edge, unable to close on a new home without occupying it that instant.

I walked these streets for hours, for days, as the local Member of Parliament, knocking on doors. Along the still-treeless boulevards carved out of corn fields and horse paddocks were homes full of people from a rainbow of countries and cultures, most with young kids. They were living amid granite countertops and marble foyers and yet often without furniture. Back in town, my office took a steady stream of calls from new residents complaining that garages were too small to actually open the doors of a mid-sized sedan when it was parked.

I also learned in my last election campaign that the biggest single political issue in this vast sprawling maze of cul-de-sacs was the hundred bucks a month parents received per child under six. So necessary was this to financial survival that my goose was cooked when the government candidate papered the dusty front doors with flyers warning my party would axe the handouts.

Scores of these rookie suburbanites bought homes they simply couldn't afford, despite the low bar in place to gain ownership. Before the federal government retracted its zero-down payment rule the day after the 2008 federal election, all Mattamy Homes required was enough actual money to pay closing costs on a new unit—typically 1.5 percent of the purchase prices, which ranged from $309,000 to $470,000.

That meant a credit card advance of $5,000 could net you a new home with stainless steel appliances, four bedrooms, a parlour, and 2,000 square feet of finished space with attached garage on a 34-foot-wide lot. Oh yes, and a $350,000 mortgage plus property taxes, utilities, insurance, and minivan payments. If you rolled this into a 40-year amortization, debt payments would be

$2,500 or so with monthly home overhead totaling about $4,000. Equity growth would be near zero, since almost all the mortgage payments were interest.

Debt without equity. Financial stress in the name of home-ownership. And sales centres parking lots were packed from fence to white picket fence each weekend, as the factory in the distance pumped out one new, no-money-down McMansion a day.

Is this now a community on borrowed time? What will these families do if the value of their homes sinks below the mortgages they struggle to service? If job loss and economic uncertainty make their incomes unstable and uncertain? If the town of Milton raises property taxes again to build new schools and swimming pools? If the minivan dies, and there's no public transit alternative to get to work? If that 40-year mortgage is reset to a 30-year amortization on renewal, jumping payments?

These are the fields of homes most at risk as real estate values erode. Unlike in more established or urban areas, here too many neighbours are in exactly the same boat—owners who are actually debtors, who'll be in negative equity soon, if it's not already dawned on them that they are. Some will stay, making payments on mortgages exceeding the worth of their properties, since they have no place else to go. Others, facing job loss in the household, will have little choice but to get out. Still others, young buyers appalled at their bad choice and scared witless at how much greater their liability could grow, will panic and bolt. Enough will choose bankruptcy over feeding the bank to earn black headlines in the *Toronto Star* about "Canada's foreclosures."

If the US experience is any guide, and it should be, every forced sale slides property values a little. In each block one or two homes might end up abandoned, their little yards filling with weeds and the front stoop incubating soggy past issues of the free weekly paper.

These suburbs in Mississauga, Calgary, Kelowna, Edmonton, Barrie, and other cities will join the crashing condos of Toronto and Vancouver to be the epicentres of the real estate-based decline that the coming years will bring. But while downtown condo values will eventually be restored, there's a good chance the suburbs will never recover. Blame that on one word, energy. When the global economy repairs and growth continues, commodity prices—including oil—will again increase to the point where the value of houses will decrease in proportion to the amount of gasoline needed to live there.

If an economic disaster looms, in other words, is there any future for suburbia, that very symbol of North America's middle class?

Back to that *Atlantic Monthly* article by Christopher Leinberger, on what might happen next:

> The experience of cities during the 1950s through the '80s suggests that the fate of many single-family homes on the metropolitan fringes will be resale, at rock-bottom prices, to lower-income families—and in all likelihood, eventual conversion to apartments.
>
> As the residents of inner-city neighborhoods did before them, suburban homeowners will surely try to prevent the division of neighborhood houses into rental units, which would herald the arrival of the poor. And many will likely succeed, for a time. But eventually, the owners of these fringe houses will have to sell to someone, and they're not likely to find many buyers; offers from would-be landlords will start to look better, and neighborhood restrictions will relax. Stopping a fundamental market shift by legislation or regulation is generally impossible...
>
> But much of the future decline is likely to occur on the fringes, in towns far away from the central city, not served by rail transit, and lacking any real core. In other words, some of the worst problems are likely to be seen in some of the country's more recently developed areas—and not only those inhabited by subprime-mortgage borrowers. Many of these areas will become magnets for poverty, crime, and social dysfunction.

Is this now the future? Will the financial contagion bring not only falling house values, rising unemployment, deflation, government deficits, plunging investments and retirement stress, but also social breakdown and a reordering of our society? After half a century of relative calm will we be huddled back into the cities? Into rugged self-reliance? Into a time of power outages, food shortages, and survival of the readiest?

Maybe. Or maybe not. Perhaps it's just extreme talk, in the age of Google, when news overwhelms us and we think we know everything. But this brings us back to the question, of what you should be doing. Everything possible? Or taking a pass?

The final section of this book is all about strategies. It's likely why you're reading it. You may not support all I have to say, but I hope you agree with this: Doing nothing is a real bad option.

As mentioned, the world is facing three serious issues, crises, actually:

- A breakdown of the economic system. A financial crisis.
- A gathering energy and climate change crisis.
- The demographic tidal wave. An age crisis.

Each one of these is tough enough to solve on its own, and requires action on the part of everyone to cope. For example, where is money possibly safe in a financial collapse? Is this 1929 all over again? What will happen to stocks, houses, bank deposits, RRSPs, jobs, pensions, or government support? Do you need to go into cash, or buy gold bullion? Where would you keep it?

With oil production hitting a peak, global demand for energy exploding, and scientists screaming about the dangers of a warming world, are you ready for gasoline rationing? Extreme weather and prolonged, widespread power outages? Electricity so expensive you'd never dream of having it on all day? Food stamps?

And as the largest generation in our history moves into

retirement age, with government already in the red, who's going to fund the health care shortfall? Are the public retirement benefits sustainable? Who'll pay for the corporate pension shortfall? How about the devaluing impact of tens of millions of Baby Boomer houses hitting the real estate market? Is this a recipe for higher taxes, deficit-crippled governments, and deflation? Where do you hide from a storm like that?

FINANCIAL CRISIS

The key to knowing what to do about money is deciding if the financial crisis is temporary insanity, or hints at something deeper.

More on how we got to this point in a few pages, but the fact is we all should have seen it coming. A society built on endless economic growth, forever-more-expensive houses, big box stores lining every highway, greed, and mounting debt just couldn't last. No other human society before us has pulled this eternal-improvement thing off.

While not part of the mainstream media, talk of a possible collapse in the financial system was around for months before it actually started to happen in the autumn of 2008. This centred on the incredible risks associated with the swapping of complicated financial assets worth hundreds of billions of dollars which were based on garbage loans arising from a bubble real estate market. Back in the summer of 2008, big banks and Wall Street brokerage firms announced they'd agreed to policy changes aimed at "easing the risk of a collapse in the $62 trillion (US) market for credit-default swaps."

The fear was that this could infect the whole banking system via big US mortgage outfits like Countrywide, which held almost 20 percent of all mortgages written in recent years. That would lead to the failure of banks and create a big mess for the Federal Reserve to deal with. As it turned out, things were much worse. Countrywide died, then the government-backed mortgage giants Fannie and Freddie failed, followed by the collapse of Wall

Street giants, the demise of several major US banks, the erasing of trillions of dollars on global markets, and a financial crisis that by the end of 2008 had seen European banks nationalized, real estate deals collapse across the globe, and countries from Iceland to Pakistan lining up for IMF bailouts.

In other words, this isn't just a financial glitch, a normal correction of overvalued markets, or a fleeting lack of investor confidence.

Far worse, and more probable: this is about the collapse of the American empire. Not good, I'd say, if your country happens to be next door and dependent on selling 70 percent of its exported goods to that one customer. This also means the current crisis is about the way we've structured the global economy—based on the bottomless future of America—and not actually the financial system. All the problems with money, markets, jobs, houses, and investments are then just symptoms.

Here's why: For years now, growth in low-wage, high-energy places like China and India has been driven by Western technology and investment. Those countries have leapt from a bad postal system to wireless in less than a decade. Companies from the US, Canada, and Europe have poured in know-how and money to build advanced factories which now supply us with everything from software to plasma TVs to PDAs and computers. We have moved high-overhead jobs from here to low-cost employees there, opening call centres to offer technical support and to manufacture at least half of everything Walmart sells in Kitchener and Abbotsford. As a result, the engine of global growth has moved eastward, where we also have an explosion in population, energy consumption, and living standards. Every single day, 14,400 new cars hit the road in China, a country which now has 49 cities each with a population of over 1,000,000.

The second key part of this is where all these products and services were aimed—which is America, of course. In 2007 alone, Americans imported $2.3 trillion worth of stuff, most of it—like laptops, cellphones, and kids' clothing—at ever-declining consumer prices, and increasingly from China. Falling prices raised US living standards, despite the irony of fewer jobs.

And while this was taking place, as Michael Mandel wrote in a late 2008 column in *BusinessWeek*, the rest of the world was lending US consumers trillions to finance the trade deficit. "The money flowed into the country in all sorts of ways, including cheap mortgages and cheap credit for cars and televisions that were made overseas. At the same time, companies in emerging markets were borrowing heavily to build the factories that were going to supply the developed world. This tri-flow worked as long as everyone believed that American consumers could finance their debt."

But, as we know now, they could not. As in Canada, the disposable income of American families has not risen enough even to match inflation for the past decade. The incredible buildup in consumer debt, credit card balances, and (especially) mortgages showed that consumerism was being financed not by income, but by credit. As borrowing increased as never before, real wages were falling and jobs were being exported—creating a campaign rallying cry for Barack Obama and raising the spectre of a new age of American protectionism.

The back-breaker may have been those subprime mortgages and their 0/40 Canadian equivalents. When they infected the housing market, they showed the only way real estate values could continue to rise was if lending standards fell, and people without money were allowed to buy in.

"Once investors started to look," Mandel observed, "they realized that the entire global edifice was built on an impossibility. The tri-flow that had built global prosperity could not be sustained. That's why the financial crisis has spread across the globe. Investors are peering at every country, from Kuwait to Korea, asking the question: Is it sound enough to survive if American demand for imports falls? The problem is in the structure of the global real economy, not the financial system."

What does this mean? Simply, that it's not going away soon. Not for years. And you'd best get ready.

ENERGY AND CLIMATE CRISIS

You might think Al Gore and David Suzuki are hucksters who have made a killing from climate change theatrics, but I wouldn't put Jacques Attali in the same category. First, he doesn't give seminars, write books, or make movies. You've never heard of him. Second, he's the former president of the European Bank for Reconstruction and Development, more concerned with the sustainable future of a continent than scaring the crap out of you. Nonetheless he does it well. Writing in the *New Statesman* as the 2008 global financial crisis grew darker, he said:

> We could find ourselves in a situation where the global increases in temperature are final and where no human action can prevent the poles from melting, the deserts from growing, the sea level from rising, or hurricanes from becoming more numerous and more powerful.
>
> Then, species of animals would disappear, life under the sea would become almost impossible, hundreds of millions of people would be forced to move, to flee deserts and coastlines, without knowing where to go. The temperature could rise so high, beyond the 4, 6, 8 degrees of which the most pessimistic hypotheses currently speak, that vast areas of the planet would become uninhabitable. Natural phenomena could disturb underwater deposits, leading to a huge release of methane into the atmosphere, asphyxiating humanity. Even the best-informed and richest would be unable to act or find refuge ...
>
> It may be an extreme hypothesis. But it is no more extreme than the hypothesis made by many economic experts in recent years, that a sub-prime crisis would lead to a general loss of control over financial derivatives—toxic or not—and to the total breakdown of interbank lending; to the weakening of hedge funds, of businesses, of nations and to the huge, lasting and uncontrollable global depression that now threatens.

This is obviously not good, and yet Attali is just giving you the broad brushstrokes of a world that lies ahead—if we wait much longer to deal with the elephant in the room. In fact, the current financial and economic meltdown could be making the coming climate crisis far worse, since we're all more worried about losing money, losing jobs and watching real estate sink, than we are about whether it rains enough in southern Alberta.

To date, we in Canada and the US have managed to all but shove two big issues off the table—our addiction to oil, which is going to run out, and our planet, which is heating up and degrading. Both countries rejected the Kyoto Protocol, neither has embraced energy conservation, and in the last election the Liberal leader and his carbon tax were kicked to the curb. In times of economic and financial stress, when families are staring at their own debt monster, the environment takes a back seat. And only when gasoline is north of $1.20 a litre, as it was through a good part of 2008, do we actually worry every day about energy.

There are few better symbols of this denial of reality than the SUV. Some time around 1990, with gas prices low and the economy growing, GM made a fateful decision: scale back on compact and fuel-efficient vehicles and go full-out with the quasi-trucks.

The gamble started to pay off by the mid-nineties and lasted for a decade. Behemoths like the Suburban, Escalade, Tahoe, and Yukon earned the company up to $15,000 a unit, and production peaked at 680,000 a year. At the same time, pickup truck sales boomed, with Silverados streaming off the Canadian production line. Never before had so many vehicles consuming so much fuel been sold to so many consumers.

The parts industry flourished, typified by Magna and a host of other companies who ringed assembly plant sites with satellite operations feeding just-in-time inventory to the voracious factories. And yet, just weeks into the market mayhem of 2008 came everyday evidence of how unsustainable the whole thing was.

Parts plants had closed, truck production collapsed, Canadian manufacturers were begging for government bailouts and GM and Chrysler were deep into merger talks—a marriage to be financed with taxpayers' money and end up in the closing of assembly plants and 35,000 fewer jobs.

This is a glimpse of what's coming. Car companies and airlines will disappear and with them armies of employees, when the next energy crisis hits. And it's not far off. Peak oil production is now behind us, which means less and less crude is being found, yet demand for the stuff spirals out of control. Billions of people in the East are becoming middle class consumers, who eat beef, not rice, and drive cars, not scooters or bicycles. The demand for oil for agriculture and transport has never been this great, and in 10 years, it will have swollen uncontrollably. Oil prices may be intensely volatile, but there's only one ultimate direction.

We face a future in which energy shortages are certain. Today most new power generating plants are fuelled by coal or natural gas, one a major emitter of greenhouse gases and the other increasingly expensive. Nuclear is an option, but radioactive waste remains a major issue, and a plant can take years to build and perfect and cost at least $7 billion a reactor. With governments in Canada and the US swimming in red ink, there's no quick fix, and little political will.

Already consumers in Ontario have lived through recent summers when electricity demand trumped capacity, resulting in brownouts. Climate change (the world is about 1 degree Celsius warmer, and heating up) will make heat waves at least twice as likely, while hitting crop yields and affecting food prices. By the way, 50,000 people died recently in heat waves in Europe, and thousands more in Chicago and New York, in two of the richest cities in the world.

Warmer weather has already helped the western pine beetle munch its way across the country, since it no longer freezes to death in winter. By 2013, 80 percent of all BC's great pine forests will be dead, and along with it the forestry industry (worth $43 billion), the many communities that depend on it, and the real estate market in every single one of them.

If you are in your twenties, by the time you are 50 the planet will be two degrees warmer. What does that mean? According to economist Nicholas Stern, who wrote a 700-page report for the British government in 2006, it means this: All glaciers will have melted, crop yields will have plunged, sea levels will have risen threatening London, New York, Cairo, and Tokyo, millions of people—environmental refugees—will be on the move, up to 40 percent of all species will have been eliminated, global financial markets will be impacted, and insurance companies bankrupted. Failure to stop this from happening, Stern says, will by then result in a 20 percent drop in the world's GDP. By comparison, economists are warning us the current downturn will be a nightmare lasting years if GDP is reduced by 4 percent.

If this doesn't have your attention, maybe this will get it. This is a story I related in *Greater Fool* about one particular day in the summer of 2003:

At 4:30 on the afternoon of August 14, I was in my office on Bay Street in downtown Toronto, adjacent to the studios in which network television shows were produced by my production company. The power failed, a very uncharacteristic event for that location. After a few minutes a camera crew which had been out on a location shoot came back to report no electricity anywhere in the downtown core.

I called my wife at our home in Caledon, a rural area about eighty kilometres away. She said the power had quit about 4:30 pm, and the generator had kicked in. That unit had been installed with some care— propane-powered, anchored in concrete, in its own building, and powerful enough to take over the entire load of our residence. I was suddenly pleased at having gone to the expense, but alarmed a power outage affecting Toronto Hydro could also have hit Ontario Hydro, our rural supplier, at precisely the same moment. Something was clearly, seriously wrong. Of course, without power there was no television, no radio, no Internet access. No information flowing into my highly-wired, high-tech office.

I left, walking down the stairwell of my building and onto the sidewalk, which was uncommonly busy. Bay Street, heading south to the expressways out of the city, was also bumper-to-bumper. But then again, it was five o'clock. Rush hour.

Reaching the parking garage I was unable to get to my car in the usual fashion, by elevator, so I walked down an exit ramp several levels until I reached it. Then, in total darkness, I threaded my way upward with a fleet of other vehicles. The streets above were now completely gridlocked, and the news blaring out of the car radio was of a massive power outage which had affected the entire eastern half of North America. It was a stunning and unprecedented event, and instilled fear. Just two years after 9/11, the obvious first thought of everyone was another terrorist attack, this time against the cables or power plants that provided energy to our modern lives and upon which we were totally dependent.

Just how dependent became apparent to me and millions of others over the next dozens of hours. Without signal lights to restrict and regulate the flow of traffic, city streets were virtually impassable. A few police were evident in some intersections, good Samaritan citizens in others, wearing fluorescent vests the cops had tossed them while driving past. Without power to many cellphone relay towers, and others overloaded, mobile phones were useless. Without functioning computers, gas stations couldn't process credit card transactions, or activate self-serve pumps. Even the most elderly of filling stations were unable to use their pumps, which employ electric motors. Without power, stores everywhere closed. Debit cards and credit cards did not work. People without cash in their pockets couldn't buy anything, nor could they obtain paper money from bank machines, which were also disabled.

Grocery stores closed immediately, unable to sell bar-coded merchandise to customers. Smokers could not get smokes, drinkers were without drinks, pets without pet food. In Toronto that day it was 88 degrees F (31C) and a whole lot hotter inside vehicles, and in office buildings with sealed windows and climate control systems. I could only imagine how it was for people trapped inside the lifts of the downtown towers.

As I inched my way towards the elevated highway out of the city centre, my partner was back in the parking garage I'd left, in the sad *realization he'd forgotten to gas up his Ford Explorer on the way in to work that morning. He ended up finding a piece of scrap garden hose and siphoning fuel out of our company station wagon after ingesting a mouthful.*

It took me three and a half hours to drive home. I was astonished to finally reach the countryside and see that every rural arterial road, line, and side road was clogged with vehicles. It was a bizarre experience to sit in a traffic jam, watching a cow. By the time I reached the village near our home the local propane company tanker truck was driving by. I flagged down the driver, whom I knew. Worried about how much gas was left in our 1,000-litre tank, I implored if he'd come over and fill them.

"Too late," he said. "Everybody's been asking, and I'm bone empty. And you can forget getting more until the power comes back on."

I made it to our gate, then rolled through the forest down the driveway towards the river, and heard the roar of the generator. My wife came out, looking vastly relieved, saying she was glad I made it home. "It feels like the world is about to change," she said. And it did. The reasons for this event were unclear. The consequences potentially dire. All I could think of was gasoline, money, food, propane. I felt under siege, and yet knew I was far better prepared than most.

With that thought, I hurried back up the hill, to the road, and padlocked the gate.

The crisis had started with tree branches in Ohio shorting out a high-voltage line, which ended up taking down the grid. It may have been a freak occurrence (or perhaps not) but it did underscore how screwed we are if the power goes out. Planes didn't fly. Trucks did not cross the border. Stores and factories, offices and banks closed. ATMs didn't work, or gas pumps, or the subway. Nobody went online.

Suddenly the most important things you could have seemed to be cash, gas, and food. After that, a generator and the fuel to run it.

If the lights went out tomorrow, for a week or a month or a year, would you be okay? Most people would be freaking.

AGE CRISIS

The third thing you need to worry about, and plan for, has no doubt of happening.

About a third of the entire Canadian population is made up of Baby Boomers, and this swarm of 9,000,000 people is rapidly entering retirement mode. Maybe. The getting old part is for sure, but leaving the work force is very much in doubt. In fact, a great number of these people stand to be chewed up the most in the financial crash currently taking place.

Boomers, more than any other group, gambled heavily on residential real estate. It's estimated that 90 percent or more of Boomer net worth is tied up in houses. The rest of it is in financial investments, like mutual funds and stocks. This is not a happy picture, is it? The real estate market is in the early stages of a US-style collapse, and stock markets have recently vaporized several trillion dollars worth of assets.

This makes it likely lots of those Boomers will have little choice but to try and dump their houses in order to raise the cash necessary to retire. The timing could hardly be worse. With the market in decline a whack of new listings will only widen the gulf between supply and demand, further crashing prices. The result will be that everybody's stress goes up as real estate goes down.

Worse, far too many Boomers own the wrong kind of real estate—big, multi-bedroom suckers in distant suburbs which suck energy and have already fallen out of favour. As a group, it's estimated this gang controls $230 billion in Canadian real estate, enough to trash our market for years to come if too much of it is bailed on.

But many people will have no choice. Over 70 percent of Canadians no longer have corporate pension plans to fall back on for cash-for-life, and the financial crisis which erupted in 2008 threatens to put even the lucky 30 percent in danger. The stock market dive took away tens of billions of dollars from pension assets companies maintain to fund obligations to former workers—

money big companies say they just can't make up. That led to a plea to Ottawa to relax the rules, giving them years more to try to fund the shortfall. It also raises the spectre of some companies going belly up over unfunded pension obligations—stiffing employees, or leaving taxpayers to bail them out.

And that, precisely, is another thing of which anyone under 40 should be wary—governments brought to their knees by the financial demands of this biggest-ever wave of retirees. Add to the pension tension the escalating cost of heath care, and we have a public finances nightmare brewing. By 2020 there will be more 65-year-old women than 14-year-old girls. The percentage of seniors is rising while the relative number of kids is dropping. This has not happened before and it's not good. Only in Japan is the demographic situation worse (and they have the real estate market to prove it).

So, who will pay for the pension bailout? The explosion in knee replacements and Viagra prescriptions? Who's going to buy all these big houses with their green swimming pools? How will governments cope? After all, Ottawa was pushed into deficit almost immediately by the current financial mess, while Washington's finances were an Iraq-induced mess even before the trillions in current bailout money was contemplated.

All of this lends more to the argument above that the American empire is fading; what we're going through now is more a global restructuring than a temporary panic; and when you add in the reality of energy crisis, climate change, and an aging population, this is way more serious than most people think.

So, are you ready?

CHAPTER TWO

"THIS IS WALMART TIME"

She's a hair stylist, a barber actually, in a joint where a clip costs about thirty bucks. Her boyfriend works in construction, and lately had a job on the Sea-to-Sky project, helping make a fluky road from Vancouver to Whistler look like a highway capable of getting tourists to the 2010 Olympic site in one piece. Together, they earn abut $100,000—when the work's steady.

Six months before the 2008 financial crisis erupted, they went to their local banker looking to get pre-authorized for a mortgage. And they did. For $900,000.

"Do you believe that?" the radio talk show host asked me before we went live in Vancouver. "I mean, she cuts my hair and they give her that kind of dough. But then, whaddya going to do? That's what houses cost."

Indeed, at that moment, the average bungalow in Vancouver had just topped the $900,000 mark, a two-bedroom condo downtown on Hornby St. was half a million (up 22 percent a year in each of three years) and the average house price as measured by the real estate board was over $750,000. How was the real estate market supposed to function, if people did not get loans to buy houses?

Three years earlier and 800 miles to the south, in an upscale suburb outside San Jose, California, John Gronley was contemplating his good fortune. The retired high-tech manager's house, bought for just over $600,000 five years earlier has just been appraised at $1.6 million, which meant his net worth had increased by seven figures—just for living there.

But before long one of his neighbours, who'd recently bought in to the Three Springs development, unexpectedly had his property go into foreclosure. The lending bank took it over, marketed it for a few months, then sold it for hundreds of thousands less than what everyone thought was fair. That one sale set a new level for comparables on the street, pulling down the market value of the entire subdivision.

But it soon became worse. Foreclosures mushroomed across California, then mortgage lenders started to fail, Wall Street went into crisis, banks collapsed, the stock market crashed, the economy choked, Washington panicked, a global recession erupted, and John Gronley's house was once again worth less than a million dollars.

"It's like play money, and I'm angry and disgusted by it," he told the local paper. "There's no accountability. And with all this creative financing, people who couldn't afford to buy in the first place got in over their heads.

"Now they're bringing everyone else down with them."

The trip up had been giddy, thrilling, and unquestioned. The trip back down was hell. After all, this wasn't supposed to happen. This was real estate. This was America.

In the autumn of 2008, the median home price in mid-state California was $308,500, down an unbelievable 33.2 percent from year-previous levels. "Falling prices will create liquidity and then a lot more people will qualify, economist Christopher Thornberg told the local press. "But in terms of recovery, we're halfway there. Prices had to fall 40 percent just to get back in line with historic norms. I think things will bottom out when they fall 50 percent."

So, welcome to our collective nightmare, unraveling in the foothills of California, near the beaches of Florida, and in unloved and unlived-in new houses in Phoenix. Now it's coming to Vancouver, Toronto, Ottawa, and Calgary where, in the final few days of 2008 there was a 223-day supply of unsold homes on the market, double the average of the previous eight years.

Where did the money come from to fuel the real estate fires?

For the Vancouver hairdresser in early 2008, from her credit union. For John Gronley's foreclosed neighbour in 2006, from a mortgage brokerage. In California they came to be called "foreclosure loans" because they were destined to fail. As one lender told the *San Jose Mercury News*, "The lender expected the borrower to lose the house and the bank would resell it for its higher appreciated value. But the market dropped and they got caught with their pants down. At least once a month we'd all look at each other and say, 'when is this bubble going to burst?' We all knew it wasn't sustainable."

And yet they lent. Why not?

House prices would go up forever. Interest rates were at a generational low in both Canada and the US, money was slopping around, and the banks were eager to write as many loans as they possibly could. Mortgage standards in both countries were relaxed and everyone, it seemed, was looking for safe, high-yield investments in the wake of 9/11 and the bursting of the tech and dot-com bubble. Real estate was clearly it.

But then something went horribly wrong, and it continues today, dooming us all to a year or a decade of losses, disappointment and—along with Mr. Gronley in Three Springs—anger and disgust.

Seven weeks before Christmas, and three weeks before the biggest shopping day of the year in the States, the second-largest consumer electronics retailer did something entirely desperate. The New York Stock Exchange had just warned Circuit City that its share price—sitting at 26 cents, after losing 96 percent of its value in the last eleven months—no longer met its requirement for continued trading. The NYSE insisted that any stock with a closing price of less than one dollar over 30 consecutive trading days would face delisting. And oblivion.

So Circuit City did what it had to. "Unprecedented events have occurred in the financial and consumer markets causing macroeconomic trends to worsen sharply," said CEO James Marcum one morning. Among those events: companies making the high-tech goodies Circuit City sold in its 700 US stores (there are another 700 in Canada) couldn't get credit from banks to make their stuff; the retailer couldn't get credit to buy it; and consumers were staying home in droves, many of them with wallets full of useless credit cards.

As a result, Circuit City closed 155 stores within four days, laid off 6,800 people, and started emergency talks with landlords to renegotiate leases on 566 more locations—downloading some of the pain and loss on to them. That immediately lopped $1.4 billion in revenue off the company's projections, created dislocation and stress for almost 7,000 families, helped depress the cash flow and value of commercial real estate, and sent out a signal that a consumer-driven economy was running on fumes.

In New York, the company's stock jumped by a third on the news. To thirty-five cents a share. One week later, the company entered into bankruptcy.

The same day, General Motors revealed monthly sales had toppled by 45 percent, the worst performance since 1975, while Ford announced its sales had collapsed by 30 percent. Toyota's numbers were off 23 percent, Honda was down 25 percent and Nissan was lower by 33 percent, with the industry on track for the worst performance in a quarter century.

"Clearly," said GM exec Mike DiGiovanni, "we're in a very dire situation. This is a severe, severe recession ... and something we really can't sustain." The company reported that light truck sales had tumbled 51 percent from previous-year levels while Ford officials said on a dismal conference call with reporters and analysts, "it's probably not the bottom." Added rival GM, "this is likely the worst month in the post-WWII era."

The industry was running on empty. Combined losses for GM, Ford, and Chrysler were $28.6 billion over just six months, while General Motors was burning through $1 billion a month. As merger talks with Chrysler went on, bankruptcy of the No.3 automaker loomed large. A report from the non-profit, Michigan-based Centre for Automotive Research warned of the effects of a complete collapse of the industry—which would cost 2.95 million jobs and $156 billion in lost taxes over three years to government.

"The collapse of the auto industry at this time," the head of Chrysler's parent company told CNBC, "would be devastating for a new president."

But that was just one of the crises confronting Barack Obama.

Home Depot, Sears, and other retailers reported they would lose as much as 8 percent of crucial holiday sales because of lenders clamping down on financing. Almost a quarter of shoppers say banks cut the spending limits on their credit cards, according to a survey by America's Research Group. More people were being rejected for new cards, hurting sales for bigger purchases. At the same time, GM's financing arm reported it was jacking up the credit requirements for people who wanted to borrow money to buy cars.

Retail sales collapsed in the wake of the stock market devastation, rising layoffs, shrinking retirement savings and the greatest number of people in 25 years claiming jobless benefits. There was only one bright spot in a withering consumer spending report: Walmart, whose aggressive cost-cutting and reliance on the cheapest of Chinese imported goods offered hope of value to cash-starved buyers. "Walmart's solid performance is reflective of the weakness in consumer spending," Ken Perkins, retail analyst, told Associated Press. "As soon as the financial crisis hit, consumer spending dropped dramatically."

That spending accounted for 68 percent of the American economy.

As Walmart president Lee Scott told retail analysts, "In my mind, there is no doubt that this is Walmart time. This is the kind of environment that Sam Walton built this company for."

Has there ever been a crash like this before? After all, consumer confidence, real estate prices, stock market values, banks, insurers, mortgage companies, jobs, car sales, and national economies all took a dive at the same time. Making it more stunning was the speed of the whole thing, which has also clouded judgments on what the hell happens next.

"As of right now, we're headed for a depression," US economist Peter Schiff concluded in late 2008, "meaning a protracted period of economic contraction with elevated levels of bankruptcies and unemployment. It is not going to be a recession the way we've come to know them."

According to Schiff, this is all the fault of one thing: debt. "If an economy lives by credit, it dies by credit. When we can't borrow any more, it implodes . . . Americans are now too broke to buy those products. We could never afford to pay for them. We were paying for them with debt."

But, says Robert Reich, Bill Clinton's secretary of labour, a university professor, and economic advisor to Barack Obama, maybe there's not enough debt, at least not enough money available to grease the economy. "The reality is that credit is not flowing," he wrote on his blog. "It's not flowing to distressed homeowners. It's not flowing to small business. It's not flowing to would-be homeowners with good credit ratings. Students are having a harder time borrowing for their tuition. Auto loans are drying up."

Reich also says the massive government response—pumping hundreds of billions of dollars into the banking system—is bound for failure. "It won't work. It can't work. The entire effort is merely saving the asses of lots of executives and traders who got us into this mess in the first place and whose asses should not be saved at taxpayer risk and expense."

On Bay Street, TD Bank economists agreed, kind of, saying

the unprecedented political action was "not a magic wand that will make the problems go away overnight. As 1,800 US banks lined up for handouts, and GM asked Washington for $25 billion to buy Chrysler, the bankers warned that more shocks could well be yet to come.

"For example, US home prices are still well above their 2003 levels—when the housing boom started—and inventories of unsold homes are running at excessively high levels, both of which point to a further decline in real estate prices in the months ahead."

In fact, more than 7.3 million American homeowners are expected to default on their mortgages by 2010, about triple the usual rate, according to Moody's Economy.com. Of those, 4.3 million are expected to lose their homes. And in Canada, who knows? The needle has just started to enter the red zone. Numbers show that people here have become every bit as indebted, and devoid of savings, as Americans.

Meanwhile the stock market collapse in Toronto as well as New York, London, and Tokyo, has made vast numbers of people less wealthy, and feeling it acutely. Chief among those are the Boomers, who control the greatest number of financial assets. That pain, says *Financial Post* Wealthy Boomer columnist Jonathan Chevreau, "has been a wakeup call for Baby Boomers who fantasized about retiring early enough to enjoy a second life.

"How does it feel to watch savings built over decades melt away in a matter of weeks? I can't speak for others but I'm upset and depressed about it because it has happened to me. The worst aspect is the self-blame, especially after hearing multiple warnings over the summer but failing to take protective measures."

Sadly, this is the generation of people who routinely invested in stocks, bonds, and mutual funds, who bought or leased new cars every three years, who had the best credit ratings, the least debt, the greatest consumer firepower, and were sitting on the bulk of their net worth in higher-end real estate. When they feel "upset and depressed" imagine the anguish among the Gen Xers, saddled with mortgage debt, the cost of young families, car loans, and suddenly uncertain economic futures. The only clear winners might be those in their twenties, the so-called Millennials, who could now contemplate buying houses and quality stocks at the biggest discount in recorded history.

"It was government intervention that created this crisis in the first place," says economist Schiff. "Interest rates came down and provided all this cheap money for everyone to speculate with."

And will it happen again? Looks like it. As Armageddon arrived, the Fed sliced interest rates to just 1 percent, from more than 5 percent a little more than a year earlier. The intent was to thaw money and unfreeze the system, while ignoring the fact exactly the same thinking had set the disaster in motion seven years earlier.

On my real estate blog, www.GreaterFool.ca, this comment was posted:

> No matter how far home prices in your area have already fallen and no matter how cheap they may appear, they could still fall a lot further. In the hardest hit regions, an individual home that was once priced for $400,000 at its peak could fall to as low as $200,000 by the end of Phase 1. But don't blindly assume that's the bottom. In Phase 2, it could fall in half again, to $100,000. And in Phase 3, it could fall by at least half for a third time, to as low as $50,000 or $40,000.
>
> Homes with peak prices of $1 million could sell for as little as $100,000; some, originally priced for $10 million may have no buyers at all—even with asking prices as low as $1 million.
>
> Nationwide, the median home price will not fall nearly that far. But that factoid alone will do nothing for homeowners in bubble areas like Florida, Nevada or California. Nor will it help those in blighted regions where factories are closed and unemployment rises far above the national average.

Never before in history have we witnessed home price declines of this magnitude! But that fact alone does not make them implausible, let alone impossible.

Remember: Never before in history has so much debt, speculation, government manipulation, fraud, corruption and consumer abuse been heaped onto any housing market! And if there's one thing that history teaches us, it's that unprecedented causes lead to unprecedented consequences.

The fear among those watching closely as 2008 ended was that we were in the early stages of a process that will roll out for years. A housing market bust, followed by a deep global recession, followed by depression and deflation. And rolling the dice in the middle of it all was the new American president, trying to distance himself from the last and making the riskiest of moves to save his fading empire.

"No amount of monetary or fiscal policy can fix the errors of the past, just like no modern treatment can quickly restore to health a drug addict debilitated from a decade-long drug abuse," wrote economist Krassimir Petrov, in the online "Market Oracle."

"Based on indicators like (1) global real estate overvaluation, (2) indebtedness, (3) leverage, (4) outstanding derivatives, (5) global bubbles, and (6) the precariousness of the global monetary system, I would argue that the accumulated imbalances in the current period surpass significantly those preceding the Great Depression. I therefore conclude that the coming US (and possibly) global depression will be of greater magnitude than the Great Depression of the 1930s. It likely suggests that we are entering a historic period that will likely be known as The Greater Depression."

But while this was happening, a conference call connecting Toronto and Ottawa linked together key players in the housing business, including Gregory Klump, chief economist for the Canadian Real Estate Association.

"The market is realigning and we don't see that there will be a housing market bust in Canada like we're seeing in the United States," said Klump. "Rather, we're going from a rather strong seller's market to more balanced market conditions." He added that home values would continue to drift lower, "until the second half of next year. With sales declining as well as listings declining, [prices] will stabilize."

So, what should we expect? Some economists say this is a recession, albeit nasty, that will be in the rearview mirror next year. Other economists warn that what's coming has all the hallmarks of a full-fledged depression, perhaps one which will make the 1930s look manageable.

If 2010 and beyond is going to bring a string of bad months, followed by recovering stock markets, improving real estate values, rising car sales, and busy malls—and you know it now—then this could pose an unprecedented buying and investing opportunity. Cheap stocks, distressed real estate prices, and a new Escalade for the price of a Chevy pickup. But on the other hand, if this is the prelude to something far more sinister, with the markets set to fall by half, houses deflating wildly, governments overwhelmed, and unemployment on its way to 20 percent, anyone borrowing or buying stands a good chance of financial oblivion.

Is that why the showrooms emptied? Why realtors started looking for other work? Why bank CEOs accepted government cash, then hoarded it? Why cars aren't selling, yet generators are flying off the shelf? Why an airline would accept only cash? Is there a growing sense that we're not in the storm, but just watching it approach?

Back in San Jose, John Gronley's local mortgage broker was asked how she could, in good conscience, make those "foreclosure loans" to people who'd have trouble ever making their mortgage payments on homes they clearly could not afford.

"I'd insist on sitting down with clients," she said, "and go through all these possible problems and frankly, people didn't want to hear it. I can't tell you how many times I heard borrowers tell me, 'God will provide.'"

Now, some economists mutter, God help us. Because never before did we get into so much trouble so fast.

As markets careened and politicians sweated, former Federal Reserve boss Alan Greenspan was summoned before a Congressional committee in September of 2008 to explain his role in the worst financial catastrophe in a generation, maybe ever. After all, he was the guy who forced interest rates down to absurdly low levels following 9/11, encouraging wild real estate speculation, then quietly urged lawmakers to ease Depression-era financial rules allowing the creation of an unregulated derivatives market that quickly came to be worth trillions.

"I made a mistake," he said, "in presuming that the self-interest of organizations, specifically banks and others, was such that they were best capable of protecting their own shareholders."

About the same time, in Iceland, the government took control of the nation's biggest lender, Kaupthing Bank, in an attempt to save the country's financial system. Iceland's banks had taken on a staggering $61 billion in debt, which was 12 times the size of the entire economy, including financing of derivatives. Days later, the island nation pleaded for an IMF bailout loan. Also about this time, executives of the world's biggest insurer, AIG—which had just accepted $85 billion in money from the US government to stave off collapse—were finishing a retreat at a luxury California resort. The company picked up the tab of more than $400,000.

So much for self-interest.

And so our story begins with Mr. Greenspan and the dot-com irrational exuberance.

In the spring of 2000, Toronto webmaster and entrepreneur William Stratas and I built a digital television broadcasting studio inside an 18-foot white cube van, hooked it up wirelessly to the Internet, parked it in downtown Toronto, and broadcast live stock market coverage and breaking business news for eight hours a day.

The timing was perfect. Daytrading was the new middle-class sport, profitless technology companies were achieving unheard-of market capitalization, and everybody wanted in on the party. While providing real time trading-based video and stock quotes to desktops everywhere, our aim was to prove TV had the ability to jump from corporate network control to the Wild West of the web. We also pioneered the first commercial use in Canada of the latest wireless technology, firing our signal from a cone bolted onto one of the truck's mirrors to a receiver mounted high atop a neigbouring office building.

That summer the young WorkdayTV.com anchors inside the vehicle parboiled. Months later they asphyxiated on fumes from a kerosene heater. "Like CNN," a *Maclean's* magazine story on the venture reported, "only cheaper." We aimed to change the nature of media coverage, and did for a few giddy months, signing up a roster of blue chip banking and brokerage accounts who handed over their television commercials to roll into our spicy stock market commentaries and man-on-the-street interviews. The first week we hit the air, I was approached by one of Canada's largest communications giants, owner of newspapers, TV stations, and magazines, desperate to have me sign a preliminary acquisition agreement.

Far too smart for that, I waited. And then the dot-com bubble burst.

The NASDAQ collapsed, ultimately losing 80 percent of its value in a spectacular erosion of wealth, sweeping away an industry built on hype, unproven ideas, investment windfalls, and no earnings. The shock hit the US and Canadian economies hard, trashing companies like Nortel, which accounted for a huge amount of the entire capitalization of the Toronto stock market. Suddenly recession loomed. Greenspan reacted, easing monetary policy and lowering the cost of borrowing to keep the economy from seizing up. His mantra, as always, was endless growth.

But scarier days were soon to come, namely September 11th

of the following year. Greenspan's Fed turned on the money taps once again in the days and months following the terrorist attacks on New York and Washington, collapsing the cost of money to a point which would not be seen again for seven years.

Traumatized by the bursting of the tech bubble and shocked at the impact of the assault on the American homeland, investors and middle-class families wondered where money might possibly be safe. And there it was: real estate. As Greenspan tackled interest rates, mortgages suddenly became generationally cheap, while the alternative—the stock market—was fraught with risk and uncertainty. Besides, buying bricks and mortar on Main Street USA was a patriotic thing to do. Soon nationalistic fervour was augmented by greed, and the next bubble was born. Real estate by the summer of 2005 was utterly, completely out of control. While the NASDAQ froth had created billions in illusionary wealth, the American housing market created trillions in new equity, all backed by an equal amount of new debt, most of it personally guaranteed by working citizens.

During this time of excess, Greenspan did two notable things.

First, he shrugged off the housing bubble. While he'd warned that the technology mania was (as he famously put it before another Washington committee) an example of "irrational exuberance" on the part of investors, when it came to a much larger, more catastrophic, real estate delusion, the Oracle (as he was called) was oddly silent. In fact, Greenspan continued to ratchet down the cost of money and mortgages until taking on new debt seemed perfectly normal. Why devote years to earning money, when you could rent a pile of it so cheaply? Why wait to have that trophy estate home in the hills overlooking the city, or put up with a less-than-gorgeous starter home, when a cheapo mortgage put it within your grasp instantly? Greenspan and his monetary policy were changing an entire culture of enterprise and saving into one of instant gratification and borrowing.

The Fed rate crashed down to the 1 percent level by mid-2004 — the cheapest money seen since the 1950s. The response was predictable. A sea of available and affordable credit spurred the demand for housing as never before, and as demand overwhelmed supply, prices soared. A new religion was born: The gospel of steadily rising assets.

By 2003 and 2004 it was ingrained into the American and Canadian populations that housing could never fall in value; that constantly increasing prices would make mortgage debt insignificant—no matter how great it might be; that first-time homebuyers would ultimately live for free because no matter what they paid, their homes would be worth more in six months. So what if young buyers of a tract home in Oakville, Ontario, bought with $5,000 down and had a $400,000 mortgage, when the place would be worth $500,000 in a year? How could it not be smart to leverage your money up by a factor of 20?

Real estate mania swept North America. In 2005, almost 1.3 million new homes were sold in the US, twice the average. In Toronto and Vancouver, it was impossible to buy a home without getting trapped in a bidding war. Prices swept higher in Calgary, Edmonton, and the suburbs around Toronto. Even markets known traditionally for cheap houses—Saskatoon and Winnipeg—launched into an unprecedented price escalation. In California, Florida, Nevada, Arizona, Washington, D.C., and the cities surrounding New York, homes that had sold for hundreds of thousands in the nineties were fetching millions in 2004. In the Greater Toronto Area, builders threw up condo projects at a furious clip, until there were—simultaneously—over 56,000 units in various stages of development.

In two and a half years the average Florida home increased in price by 227 percent, and yet all Alan Greenspan would say when asked about it was that there was "a little froth" and "... it's hard not to see that there are a lot of local bubbles". (It would not be until 2008 that the former Fed chief, then promoting his memoirs, admitted that when it came to the greatest financial bubble in history, "I really didn't get it until very late in 2005 and 2006.")

Even as the excess reached its later stages—with the greatest price increases coming on falling sales volumes—the housing industry vehemently denied the existence of an unsustainable market. The chief economist of Freddie Mac said, flat out, no big price decline was in the cards for American real estate since it had never happened since the Great Depression. Insatiable Boomers, he declared, and healthy employment, will keep real estate alive. In the summer of 2005, the National Association of Realtors attacked those warning that the party was about to end, distributing Anti-Bubble Reports which mocked "the irresponsible bubble accusations made by your local media and local academics."

"People should not be concerned that home prices are rising faster than family income," the NAR said. "There is virtually no risk of a national housing price bubble based on fundamental demand for housing and predictable economic factors." So much for corporate responsibility.

After all, the North American real estate orgy was clearly out of control. In Vancouver the average home price topped $700,000 for the first time in 2007. In California, the median home price increased from $372,700 to $524,000 in just three years. (In 2008 it would come crashing back down to $283,000, as 51 percent of all sales ended up being foreclosures.) For the first time in recorded history, at the peak of the housing bubble, average home prices hit five times the annual income of owners, while affordability crashed to the lowest level ever. And yet, the orgy continued, floated on an endless sea of debt.

As US investment guru Martin Weiss pointed out:

Once set in motion, the speculative fever spread quickly. From Miami to Phoenix to San Diego to Las Vegas, investors camped outside housing developments to snap up three, four, five, or more units at a time. Condominium developers built gleaming towers in major cities, based almost exclusively on anticipated bids from investors and speculators and with no evidence of real underlying demand. From coast to coast, investors signed on to millions of pre-construction contracts, only to flip them before the first shovels touched the ground.

This kind of speculation was traditionally just a small niche in the giant US housing market. But at the peak of the housing boom, it nearly took over: An astounding 40 percent of houses and condos were bought as second homes or investments. The yearly rate of appreciation on existing homes catapulted from 3.6 percent in January 2001 to 16.6 percent in November 2005. On new homes, meanwhile, it surged from 4.8 percent in to 18.1 percent.

Despite Greenspan's cheap money, as prices soared real estate became less affordable, slipping away from middle- and lower-income families who wanted their piece of the North American dream but no longer qualified for enough debt to get it. So, to keep the party going, mortgage lending standards plunged. Creative financing erupted. The debt spiral intensified, sucking in millions of families who gave scant thought to a nightmare scenario. What if the market crashed?

To qualify new buyers, sellers started paying closing costs. Deals based on 100 percent financing suddenly became commonplace. Mortgages were given to small business owners, commission salespeople, and others with uneven earnings, without proof of income. "Liar loans," the industry called them. There were those Ninja loans, extended to people without cash, incomes, visible employment, or assets but who, as one mortgage broker famously said, "could fog a mirror." Mortgages with low introductory rates—"sucker loans"—emerged, and borrowers readily took them, fully expecting rising house values would allow them to tap into increased equity when the loan was reset at a higher rate, and pay down the principal. At least, that's what they were told to expect by a mortgage brokerage industry in its golden age.

As they did in Canada, interest-only mortgages hit the marketplace, allowing borrowers to rent money without actually paying any of it back. Every month, cash went out the door and yet no equity was built. Just like rent. But unlike rent, there was a whopping mortgage that—at some point—would have to be repaid. Worse, lenders allowed homeowners to make partial monthly payments which did not even cover the interest owed, simply adding the shortfall to the mortgage principal. This meant the debt grew steadily larger, families sank deeper into the red, and when housing prices started to drop, it all but guaranteed financial failure.

Much of this lending fell into a broad category of junk loans known as "subprimes." By 2006, 13.6 percent of all outstanding mortgages in the US were subprime, according to the Mortgage Brokers Association. But added to that were conventional mortgages in deals where no-money-down financing had been involved and the buyers closed on properties in which they had no equity, only expectations.

But crap mortgages, irresponsible consumer information, and the outright greed of lenders, sellers, and buyers leading to an unstable and unsustainable bubble were not the only financial misdemeanors Alan Greenspan overlooked. As real estate values soared, every homeowner felt wealthier, and consumer spending increased. Why save, after all, when your house was making more money every month than you possible could? Why not go for the RV, flat screen TV, or cottage you'd always wanted?

Home equity loans, known as "refis" or refinancings, swept America. Tens of millions of households tapped into their newly-created equity, converting a paper gain into real cash backed at the same time by real debt. This literally created billions of new dollars which then flowed into the consumer economy, feeding growth and expansion and allowing the entire cycle to continue.

The amount borrowed, and spent, was staggering. According to the US central bank, in 2005, American homeowners took $750 billion out of the equity in their homes, and spent two-thirds of it on consumer toys, vacations, home improvements, or more real estate. The sudden avalanche of money helped breed a cult of real estate, and the immense popularity of housing-related television programs, like *This Old House, Holmes on Homes, Property Virgins,* and *Flip this House,* and entire networks such as Home and Garden Television.

Of course, equity borrowing was as dangerous as loading up on rising stocks using a margin account, or borrowed money. Market gains exaggerated profits, while losses were amplified. But few Americans in the years following 9/11 thought a declining housing market was remotely possible. Lost was logic. Gone was the guiding hand and supposed sage moderation of America's central banker, considered after the president to be the most powerful man in Washington.

Then, the bad lending practices of an out-of-control lending industry were sucked into the vortex of government finance. In 2005 and the two years following, Fannie Mae, one of the two federally-created mortgage giants, purchased or guaranteed $270 billion worth of subprime home loans, generating bonuses for senior execs of up to $90 million. Three years later, Fannie and its companion Freddie Mac were bankrupt—their stock having lost 90 percent of its value—and Washington was forced to spend $100 billion on each just to keep them afloat.

Through it all, Greenspan watched this spawning of toxic mortgage assets leading to the creation of the greatest financial bubble in history and did nothing. Said nothing. Even when it was obvious the real problem was that average families could no longer afford the average home on the average income, without resorting to unprecedented levels of debt at unsustainably low rates.

How could this not end badly?

But it was about to get worse. Far worse.

Meanwhile in conservative Canada, as mentioned, we were doing exactly the same thing. Real estate values soared as the Bank of Canada slavishly followed the course of US interest rates. Mortgage carrying costs plunged, borrowing exploded, home loan debt rocketed by $100 billion and house prices increase by 73 percent in the six years following September 11th, 2001.

As affordability levels slipped, threatening the real estate gravy train, Ottawa gave in to industry demands and allowed a northern version of subprimes to be created. In late 2006, mortgage repayment periods started to expand to 40 years from the traditional 25, with the effect of dropping monthly payments. This meant more buyers could afford to carry big debts and that purchasers could qualify for heavier debt on the same income—allowing house prices to rise further. At the same time, through Canada Mortgage and Housing, the government gave its blessing to no-money-down purchasing with its guarantee of 100 percent financing. Suddenly people without money could buy houses worth a half million dollars.

By the time the 0/40 mortgages, as they came to be known, were recognized as the same destructive, bubble-creating instruments as the subprimes which had crashed the US middle class, it was too late. Ottawa banned them in mid-October, 2008, when the Canadian housing market was entering the freefall I had predicted in *Greater Fool* earlier that year. At that time, it appeared certain the US housing crash which had started in the autumn of 2006 was just beginning, and Canadians would soon have to endure the pain they'd watched unfold to the south of them for two years, in detached fascination.

But while Main Street was gorging itself on granite countertops, stainless appliances, gated communities, bamboo flooring, and views, Wall Street—thanks to the cagey Fed boss—was engaged in activity which would ultimately rock the entire global economy.

How did giving loans to un-creditworthy people so they could buy homes they couldn't afford in the suburbs of San Francisco and Mississauga come to bankrupt Iceland? And destroy Merrill Lynch? Make Barack Obama president? Threaten a world depression?

In simplest terms, Wall Street investment bankers took hundreds of thousands of those residential mortgages and bundled them together into a new kind of financial security known as CDOs — collateralized debt obligations. They were then sold to investors individually, to other financial institutions, to municipal boards and pension administrators all over the world, and to domestic and international hedge funds. And everybody wanted them, of course. Why not? They were based on one of the best investments possible—residential mortgages of hard-working entrepreneurial middle-class Americans. They paid a handsome rate of return. And they carried blue chip ratings from the best-known agencies like Moody's and Standard & Poor's.

Bankers profited on the difference in interest they were getting from the mortgages, and the yield being paid to CDO investors. That meant the financial institutions made money on the mortgage loan, then more money selling the mortgage, and received a revenue stream they could re-loan. Investors got a solid asset paying a premium rate. Mortgaged homeowners got houses they didn't merit financially. What wasn't to like?

Soon the CDOs were getting more exotic, and being bundled in with car loans, credit card debt, and commercial real estate mortgages. The market they traded in was virtually unregulated and global in nature. But it was all about to get worse.

A year or two before the housing bubble burst, some smart people saw the inevitable coming. They created a new security, a form of insurance, called credit default swaps, which acted in a similar way to shorting a stock—or wagering that shares would decline in value. These guys bet against all those mortgages, on the premise that homeowners in large numbers would soon start to default on their payments, turning the CDOs toxic. Insurance companies which traded in credit default swaps were betting home values would continue to rise, and the mortgages stay solid.

When the housing market began to tank, the insurers were faced with staggering liabilities. As a wave of mortgage defaults and foreclosures swept America, the mortgage-backed securities and CDOs became increasingly worthless, and the swaps so huge they couldn't all be honoured. The banking system began to freeze up, credit tightened, and that caused increased housing market turmoil, with falling prices, more foreclosures, and a further crash in real estate values. That made it impossible for many people to pay off their lines of credit or refinancings, while millions more suddenly owed more than they owned, and walked away from their homes. A crisis had turned into a catastrophe, and dominoes started to skid out of place all over the world.

Now, back to Greenspan, who was well aware of the emerging credit default swaps, which were a form of the derivatives he had defended in Washington for years. (Derivatives are products that "derive" their value from underlying assets—in this case, residential mortgages. They are used as a "hedge" which means a way to soften potential losses on investments.)

Greenspan liked an active derivatives market because it formed part of an alternative banking system providing trillions of dollars to the economy and which he believed would be ultimately self-regulating. But hedging through derivatives also allowed financial companies to take more involved risks than they normally would. The derivatives contracts were themselves securities which were traded, an activity which hugely increased the number of investors—private and corporate—exposed to ruin if the underlying assets went bad.

And, of course, they did. Big time.

It wasn't like this was a surprise, either. The US Congress had been trying to regulate the derivatives business for years, but Greenspan just outfoxed the lawmakers. Back in 1994 the head of Washington's accounting office had told a Congressional committee, "The sudden failure or abrupt withdrawal from trading of any of these large US dealers could cause liquidity problems in the markets and also pose risks to others, including federally insured banks and the financial system as a whole."

In 2003 no less a man than legendary investor and billionaire

Warren Buffet cautioned his shareholders, "Large amounts of risk, particularly credit risk, have become concentrated in the hands of relatively few derivatives dealers. The trouble of one could quickly infest the others."

Greenspan responded by saying derivatives were useful, since they spread the risk. What he failed to understand, amazingly, is that they also shared the pain, magnified the losses,and had the potential to bring the world to a fateful weekend exactly seven years after his greatest triumph—the survival of the market after 9/11.

What terrorists could not do to America, Americans did to the world.

In the Internet age, everything is time-compressed. Even a global financial meltdown. In fact, the very way we communicate is greasing the trip down. During the Great Depression and into the Second World War, North Americans waited patiently to hear one of 28 "fireside chats" on the radio, delivered over 11 years by Franklin D. Roosevelt.

In the Internet age of 2008, George W. Bush addressed the American people on the subject of the financial meltdown on live TV and via the web on September 24, then through televised news conferences on Sept. 25, Sept. 26, Sept. 29, Sept. 30, Oct. 2, Oct. 6, Oct. 9 and in another speech to the country, delivered from the Rose Garden of the White House, on October 10th. That was followed by Presidential remarks on the faltering economy on Oct. 11, Oct. 13, Oct. 14, Oct. 15, Oct. 17, and Oct. 20.

The guy could not keep quiet, and yet the constant reassurances and dialogue did nothing to stem the tide of negative news, market losses, and sense of drift. Suddenly too much information only served to accelerate the decline—a lesson presidents may have forgotten.

On March 12, 1933, after he had ordered the country's banks shut following a panicked run on deposits, FDR said:

We had a bad banking situation. Some of our bankers had shown themselves either incompetent or dishonest in their handling of the people's funds. They had used the money entrusted to them in speculations and unwise loans. This was of course not true in the vast majority of our banks but it was true in enough of them to shock the people for a time into a sense of insecurity and to put them into a frame of mind where they did not differentiate, but seemed to assume that the acts of a comparative few had tainted them all. It was the Government's job to straighten out this situation and do it as quickly as possible—and the job is being performed.

On September 24, 2008, after he had proposed an historic $700 billion "rescue plan" for the economy, GWB said:

The government's top economic experts warn that without immediate action by Congress, America could slip into a financial panic, and a distressing scenario would unfold: More banks could fail, including some in your community. The stock market would drop even more, which would reduce the value of your retirement account. The value of your home could plummet. Foreclosures would rise dramatically. And if you own a business or a farm, you would find it harder and more expensive to get credit. More businesses would close their doors, and millions of Americans could lose their jobs. Even if you have good credit history, it would be more difficult for you to get the loans you need to buy a car or send your children to college. And ultimately, our country could experience a long and painful recession.

In the depths of the Great Depression, FDR's words and actions aside, the forces of the economy would continue to chew up families for another seven years, until the war effort stimulated production.

Would Bush be any more successful? Could he have been any less so?

- February 2008: After being a willing buyer of hundreds of billions worth of mortgage-backed securities, and in the middle of a wave of mortgage defaults and foreclosures, government-backed Fannie Mae reports a $3.5 billion quarterly loss, three times what had been expected. Its stock loses 80 percent of its value.
- March: Unknown to most of its clients, Wall Street investment bank Bear Stearns teeters on the brink of collapse, and accepts a buyout from rival JP Morgan Chase. Washington backs the deal with $30 billion in loans. Meanwhile in Germany, giant Deutsche Bank reveals a quarterly loss of 141 million euros, the first in half a decade. In Washington, another $200 billion is quietly injected into Fannie Mae and Freddie Mac.
- April: G7 ministers meet to discuss a growing financial crisis. The International Monetary Fund warns of potential losses of $945 billion.
- June: Statistics reveal the pace of home repossessions in the US is nearing epidemic proportions. Bear Stearns executives are charged with mortgage fraud.
- July: The first major consumer bank bites the dust. California-based mortgage lender IndyMac abruptly closes its doors, laying off half its staff: 4,000 people. The bank was on the hook for billions in mortgage loans, mostly in an area where real estate values had fallen by 40 percent. Fannie and Freddie continue to disintegrate as the federal government moves to guarantee their debts—a move aimed at stemming a stock market meltdown. President Bush tells the country to "have confidence in the mortgage markets." In Spain, the country's largest real estate developer goes belly up.
- September 7: Washington seizes control of Freddie and Fannie.

- September 14: Wall Street investment bank Lehman Brothers files for bankruptcy during a weekend of financial shocks. At the same time, rival Merrill Lynch agrees to be taken over by Bank of America.
- September 16: The next domino falls, as the world's largest insurer, AIG (American International Group) hits the skids. Washington announces an $85 billion loan in return for an 8 percent stake in the company. In Britain, Barclays Bank buys part of Lehman's North American assets for just under $2 billion.
- September 17: Britain's largest home loan lender, shaken by plunging real estate values and mortgage delinquencies, is taken over by Lloyds Group.
- September 18: A temporary ban is imposed on short-selling in several financial centres, including New York and London, to try and staunch market blood.
- September 19: US Treasury Secretary Henry Paulson reveals Washington has a plan to take over hundreds of billions of dollars in bad-credit mortgages, wiping them off the books of troubled banks. Stock markets soar on the prospect of massive government intervention, The Dow rises the greatest amount since 1933.
- September 20: Details of the $700 billion rescue package are made public. The amount seems staggering.
- September 21: Goldman Sachs and Morgan Stanley, the only remaining giants of the five Wall Street investment banks, become bank holding companies, now far more tightly regulated by the federal government.
- September 25: The largest bank failure in US history takes place as Washington Mutual (WaMu) is closed by the federal government. Its banking assets are sold to JPMorgan Chase for pennies on the dollar.
- September 29: Major British mortgage lender Bradford & Bingley is nationalized by the UK government to prevent its collapse. On the European continent, bank and insurance giant Fortis is bailed out of a near-collapse by the Belgian and

Dutch governments for $16 billion. In the US, Wachovia bank avoids closing by agreeing to sell most of its assets to Citigroup in a deal engineered by federal regulators. The US House of Representatives shockingly rejects passing the White House bailout package, reflecting massive public resentment against a rescue for Wall Street while Main Street suffers. In New York, Toronto, and other financial centres, stock markets crater. The Dow has its worst day since Black Monday, 1987.

- September 30: Stock markets around the world tank on fears of a global financial meltdown.
- October 1: The US Senate hastily passes a revised version of the bailout package, which has blossomed from a three-page bill to a volume of more than 400 pages. European lenders contemplate a 300 billion-euro bailout plan of their own.
- October 3: The British government follows the lead of Washington, moving to stem a run on the banks by jacking up deposit insurance for consumers. The move is repeated two days later in Germany.
- October 7: A popular bank in Iceland blocks savers from their own money.
- October 8: Central banks in the US, Canada, Britain, and Europe slash interest rates in the first concerted move since 9/11. This is followed in the next four weeks by a string of rate cuts which will ultimately reduce borrowing costs to 1 percent in the States and just a third of a point in Japan.
- October 9: The Dow loses another 7 percent, dropping to a five-year low. House prices in Britain are revealed to have plunged 13 percent in a year.
- October 10: The Dow crashes 700 points in just minutes. The Japanese market loses 10 percent of its value, the largest drop in 20 years. Oil prices slump to a point where they are 50 percent less than just four months earlier. President Bush urges confidence, and is ignored.
- October 11: G7 finance ministers assemble in Washington and

come up with a vague five-point plan. The head of the IMF tells them, "Intensifying solvency concerns about a number of the largest US-based and European financial institutions have pushed the global financial system to the brink of systemic meltdown."

- October 13: Stocks soar on renewed hopes government will paper over problems with public money. The Dow gains 936 points, or 11 percent or the biggest advance in history. Skeptics call it a dead cat bounce, which turns out to be correct.

- October 15: Iceland tries to stave off disaster with an unprecedented 3.5 percent interest rate cut, while talking to Russia about a bailout loan.

- October 19: Dutch banking giant ING gets a 7 billion-euro bailout from the government of the Netherlands.

- October 22: Chicago-based Wachovia bank reports the biggest quarterly loss of the crisis: $24 billion.

- October 23: Former Fed boss Alan Greenspan admits he was wrong in handling the housing bubble and the banking industry. He tells a Congressional committee the credit crunch has him in "shocked disbelief." News comes that one in five Americans now has negative equity in their home.

- October 28: Financial system losses so far, says the Bank of England, total almost $3 trillion.

- October 29: Washington oversees a bank rate cut to just 1 percent, amid speculation that the cost of money for the first time ever may hit zero. Days later Britain shocks markets by dropping its lending rate by 1.5 percent.

- November 4: Barack Obama is elected President on the themes of change and hope.

- November 5: Obama's spokesman tells the *New York Times* that Americans would be wrong to see the new president "as a miracle worker who in two months is going to solve an economic crisis."

Even in the Internet age, for an Internet president who raised

$600 million online, there are forces beyond controlling.

IT'S NOT OVER YET. IS NEGATIVE EQUITY COMING?

Trillions of dollars were spent by governments trying to stem the damage caused by the real estate bubble that started in America, then spread to Canada, Europe, and most of the developed world. Never before had governments reacted so quickly, so massively, in such a concerted way. Bank deposits were guaranteed, lenders nationalized, interest rates plunged simultaneously, and vast amounts of money were found overnight.

This should worry you. A lot. Because you may think this crash is over, but it isn't yet.

The residential housing market is the largest financial game on the planet. Nothing else comes close. For example, the $4.8 trillion in US mortgages bundled into securities and sold around the world represented just a fraction of the American housing debt, and yet was worth 60 percent more than all the stocks listed in the Dow Jones Industrial Average.

There isn't enough money in Washington to even start repairing the damage caused by the speculative bubble which exploded with such force. And there's good reason to believe we're nowhere near a bottom, despite all the reassurances central bankers and elected politicians might manufacture.

For example, the West Coast—British Columbia and California. What happened in California likely foreshadows by two years events that BC can expect, and it's not a pretty picture. Half of all late 2008 home sales were distressed, abandoned, or repossessed properties, at fire sale prices. As mentioned, the median house price dropped by half in three years, retracing all of its previous gain. But pendulums seldom stop in the middle, and the middle class is entirely stressed out and over-indebted after the housing orgy. So, expect more.

In 2009, the inventory of unsold homes in the queue is extreme, and buyer confidence has withered. Interest rates in both Canada and the US have collapsed with central banks doing all they can to encourage new borrowing and renewed buying. But as those key government rates dropped, mortgage costs hardly budged. Lending has choked up again, and the reason is simple.

After the crash of 2008, bankers are back to doing what we all thought was normal—checking credit ratings and borrowers' incomes, appraising houses, requiring down payments and making prudent loans to people with the ability to pay them back. Surprisingly, the average family still cannot afford the average home.

In California, the median income is a little over $60,000 and the average home price (even after falling by half) is around $300,000. With just a 10 percent down payment, that family would need $30,000 in hand, which would mean saving $2,500 a month for a year—two-thirds of net income. That's not going to happen. But if it did, the mortgage would cost $1,800 a month (30-year fixed rate loan), and carrying the house would be at least $2,500, again more than 60 percent of net income.

In a recession, with job losses mounting, wages falling and deflationary pressures abounding, is that likely? Is carrying a house worth two-thirds of your income? Is lending that amount prudent? Is the mortgage safe from default? Is the underlying asset—the house—likely to keep falling in value until it becomes more affordable to a greater pool of buyers?

Now, how about Vancouver, where the average house is still over $700,000, and yet the average family makes little more than in the state to the south? Is there any doubt what's coming? How can homes sell in the Lower Mainland for ten times the annual income, when the California bubble burst at half that ratio? And how about Toronto, far more affordable than Vancouver, but where the average home sat at $375,000 in late 2008 (after a 15 percent decline), and the median family income was $75,000, or one-fifth the cost of that property?

To buy such a house with 10 percent down takes $47,000 in cash (including land transfer tax to the province and city), and

$2,900 a month in mortgage and property tax (five-year rate of 7.2 percent with 25-year amortization). With insurance and utilities, that comes to about $3,800 a month, or $45,600 a year. But the after-tax net income of that family in Ontario is just $57,000— leaving a scant $11,400 a year, or $220 a week, for everything else, including food and fuel.

In other words, for the average family to buy the average-priced home in Toronto, which is far from the country's priciest housing market, at the end of 2008 required savings of $47,000 (when the national savings rate is zero) plus 61 percent of gross family income, and 80 percent of after-tax, actual income.

What? Why would families take on such a crippling obligation? Especially at a time when deflation is settling in and real estate values are certain to fall? The only possible justification for devoting 80 percent of what you have in your paycheque to one asset is if you think it'll rise in value, giving a tax-free capital gain. But does anyone still believe that?

I hope not. Because the opposite's destined to occur.

Real estate must return to the point where average families have a reason to buy a home, and can do so without crippling their budgets. Otherwise renting is a far superior option. That means getting back to the days where 15 percent down could put you into a home which roughly a third of your gross income could carry (mortgage and property tax).

Figure it out. For the average Canadian urban household making $75,000, that's a house worth no more than $270,000, suggesting Toronto prices are too high by more than $100,000 and Vancouver is overpriced by a stunning $430,000.

Is a drop in average prices of that magnitude even possible? On the other hand, if prices don't fall to the point where Canadians can afford to buy them, who will? How can there be a market without buyers? As listings mount and desperate sellers wait months and months to unload, as supply trumps demand, aren't lower prices inevitable?

And as current over-valued housing stock in Canadian cities

plunges, existing mortgage debt remains. That could doom millions of families in BC, Alberta, and Ontario especially with negative equity in 2010 and 2011, before this market finds a bottom.

The Crash of 2008, as traumatic, fast-paced and stunning as it was, could well be a prelude to one, or both, of the following chapters:

- Higher unemployment, corporate failures, a recession, and deflation.
- Credit drought, real estate collapse, a bear stock market, depression.

More on those possible scenarios in a few pages, plus some suggestions on what any of us might do to protect our families and our money, and a look back to see what people did when faced with a similar situation. As you know, there was a Depression 70 years ago, but in that one crashing real estate was the result of a stock market rout, bank failures, and millions of lost jobs. This time real estate was the catalyst, which has ironically created those conditions (loss of jobs, restricted credit, contracting economy, eroding family finances) which led in the 1930s to a massive housing deflation.

Does this mean the spiral in the value of our homes experienced to date is just a precursor to a more substantial correction—down to the values mentioned above, where it's once again affordable to most? This is actually a distinct possibility because, simply put, we've never screwed up this badly before.

The world has gone through other bubbles, which had dire results. Stock investors in the Depression lost almost 90 percent of their money. Investors in the tech-heavy NASDAQ in 2000 and 2001 were cleaned of 80 percent of their cash. Japan's 15-year-long bear market also took more than 80 percent of invested wealth. The gold boom and bust of twenty-five years ago saw 70 percent declines.

But in each of those there were vast differences from the housing-induced Crash of 2008 (and beyond). Those earlier losses were contained to people with direct exposure—to stocks or bullion. Despite the common myth that everybody in the 1920s was a stock speculator, the fact is that less than 7 percent of the population was touched by the initial event. It was the consequences later which had the real impact on society.

The cause of today's crash was not just a rerun of the same wild speculation, greed, and irresponsible behaviour of the past, but also debt. Bad debt. And debt that underlay the biggest single market on the planet—residential real estate.

After all, this is what our Canadian and American banks did:

- They allowed no-money-down purchasing of houses. Even Canada Mortgage and Housing Corporation approved a 100 percent financing program, which meant that people who couldn't walk out of a Future Shop with a free thousand-dollar plasma television could buy a new home in a Toronto suburb worth $450,000—for nothing.
- They worked with developers using federal government regulations to leverage up no-money-down real estate. For example, a young couple would be given money by a real estate marketing company to invest in an RRSP account at a bank. Upon closing their real estate deal 90 days later they could withdraw the funds tax-free, pay back the developer, and use their tax refund to close the deal. The bank might also loan the original funds to the developer.
- They let consumers finance all the purchase price of a home, providing 100 percent leverage, whereas anyone wanting to borrow money to buy stocks would need at least 50 percent cash. Those wishing to borrow money to acquire or start a business and hire employees were out of luck.
- They allowed borrowers to make interest-only payments on

mortgages, turning homeowners into renters with debt they obviously could not repay.

- They extended mortgages to people without income verification. In the US they were called liar loans. In Canada one bank labeled them "self-employed recognition mortgages." (This description is from the CIBC mortgages website: "Approval is based on your self-declared income, strong equity, and excellent personal credit history. Best of all, you don't need to prove your income.")
- They extended repayment terms to four decades, lowering monthly payments by vastly increasing the amount of debt to be repaid and the interest owing.
- They approved mortgages without physically looking at the property. Canadian banks routinely gave thumbs up after only researching a postal code.
- They gave loans to borrowers who qualified only for low introductory below-prime (subprime) rates, knowing full well those rates would likely be reset in several years at a much higher level, risking default. And that is just what happened.
- They bundled these mortgages, sold them to investors around the world, and thereby stopped caring if they were ever repaid or not. They were then someone else's problem.
- They gave hundreds of thousands of dollars to hairdressers along with the reinforcement that buying a house was a smart thing to do, even when it cost the better part of a million dollars. Even when they knew that debt was probably unserviceable.

In that, our bankers—together with real estate agents, brokers and local board officials, real estate marketing companies, housing industry officials, bank economists, and the media which blindly and irresponsibly pumped them up—let these people down. If I'm right in my suspicions, they've also condemned these Canadians to years of financial hardship, as the value of their properties sink well below the loans they took to buy them.

Soon hundreds of thousands of Canadians will learn there is no "jingle mail" in Canada. It's not possible to put your house keys in an envelope, mail them back to the bank, and walk away as so many Americans have done. While "short selling" is a common practice in the US, letting homeowners with negative equity just transfer their problems to the bank (but with some personal tax liability), in this country you're liable for every dollar of the mortgage. Miss some payments, and you'll also be on the hook for fat legal fees. Take a walk and you can expect to have your property sold under power of sale, and to be sued at the same time for the entire amount of the debt.

There is much blame to go around, as we stare into an uncertain future. So many of us have made poor decisions, based on advice and information which turned out to be both wrong and self-dealing.

In the final days of 2008, for example, came word that housing sales and prices in the Toronto area were taking the biggest hit in years. Sales plunged by 35 percent from year-previous levels, while the average house price dropped by 10 percent, after suffering a 15 percent annualized decline the month earlier. The median value of a home in the GTA was actually less than it had been two years earlier, while sales had dropped to a six-year low.

When I had warned of exactly this potential nine months earlier, the *Toronto Star* ran a full-page review of my book, *Greater Fool*, noting:

> But try to find a respected Canadian economist who buys into Turner's pessimism. People at the University of Toronto's economics department, the Ivey School of Business at the University of Western Ontario, and the University of British Columbia's Centre for Urban

Economics and Real Estate couldn't find one for us. While most seem to think a gradual softening is likely after 10 years of constant price increases, a US-style meltdown doesn't appear to be on anyone's radar.

"I think you will have a very tough time finding any economists who agree with Turner on this," says Tsur Somerville of UBC.

Gilles Duranton of the University of Toronto is not keen on long-term predictions, but can't see any circumstances likely to cause a significant downturn in the next six months. "There are sometimes bubbles waiting to burst," he says, "but nothing indicates the Toronto market is bubbly."

It was exactly words like what which encouraged Canadians to keep on buying new homes with nothing down, lining up to buy un-built condos, taking out 40-year mortgages, and engaging in bidding wars for overpriced houses, all while the US middle class was being decimated by a real estate crisis. How could such smart people be so dumb?

And the spin did not even stop when the first irrefutable indications came that Canadian housing would follow a similar track to that in the States. As those dismal Toronto sale and price statistics were being announced, the president of the local real estate board, Maureen O'Neill said, "There's no doubt that real estate will continue to be a solid long-term investment in our country."

Sharing the blame must be the regulators and the politicians, including Alan Greenspan, who created the conditions in which a real estate bubble could be formed, and then abdicated their responsibility to regulate a marketplace out of control. Subprime lending was a crime against the consumer, while derivatives, swaps, and mortgage-backed securities were lethal to the financial system and, in the process, killed trust.

Of course, real estate consumers—homebuyers and borrowers, those sellers who encouraged bidding wars, and people using their home equity like bank machines—are far from blameless. We all encouraged a tidal wave that raised every boat.

These actions, among others, ensured that this most recent crash would be the most pervasive and far-reaching in history. They undermined the financial foundation of the real estate sector. They invited losses, defaults, and failures. They attacked the root of family wealth in Canada and the US. And they spread toxic non-performing debt around the world, with grave consequences for the financial system we all depend upon.

And this is why we're far from done.

CHAPTER THREE

FROM SAFES TO SQUIRRELS

It happened first at Home Depot stores across North America. Quietly, without any marketing hoopla, promotions or reduced prices, home safes started to fly off the shelves in the last few months of 2008. By the time the new American president was taking office, as the stock market was tanking and the latest corporate news just awful, it seems a lot people were voting for something truly hopeful: cash.

The first reports of people lugging 600-pound safes home in their cars came on a public radio broadcast in September, 2008. Then it spread to upstate New York, Kansas City, Seattle, Los Vegas, Memphis, and across California. Without any media scrutiny, the worried rebellion was already infecting Ontario, as quickly as the economic backbone of the auto industry seemed to be crumbling.

"People are starting to wake up," a former mortgage broker told Bloomberg. "They don't believe the lies coming out of Wall Street. There's a lot of fear out there."

And why not?

A total of 15 US banks had just failed, while mutual fund and insurance companies in Canada started to wobble and the prime minister mused about the need for a direct cash infusion into our banks, just two months after a federal election in which voters were told the banking system was the most sound in the world.

Questions. It all raised doubts about what, or who, to believe.

The biggest bank failure in American history took place during the crash of 2008, while more than a hundred others were on Washington's list of potential casualties. This scenario of people trusting their own homes more than the corner bank was exactly what governments around the world feared most. It's why they scrambled to raise deposit insurance, then make sure citizens knew about it.

But that didn't seem to matter to some folks in my town. After I read about the run on safes, I got on my bike and visited two nearby Home Depots. Both were safe-less. "Backordered," I was told, "but forget it. They're already all spoken for."

"Whatever money you may need for the next five years," said CNBC *Mad Money* host Jim Cramer on network television as the Dow plunged, "please take it out of the stock market right now." The next day, Washington announced that deposits in banks would be protected up to $250,000—a quantum leap from the former $100,000 limit. The move was matched in Britain, France, Italy, and other jurisdictions—but not Canada.

The largest safe manufacturer in the world is SentrySafe, which was reporting a sales surge of as much as 70 percent by the end of the year at some retailers, and a one-month increase of 40 percent in October—a time when the stock market took its worst hit since the early 1930s. The reason, company CEO Jim Bush said, seemed obvious: people were losing faith in the banks. California safe maker Cannon Safe echoed the sentiment, with president Aaron Baker saying he expected a 30 percent hike in business during 2009. "Whenever there's an economic downturn, safes tend to sell very well." Said a Home Depot employee in Washington State, where safe sales were ahead 27 percent, "I think it's a government trust thing. They're not quite sure it's really going to be there or not."

Why hoard cash?

If you believe there's a chance the recession could become depression, or worse, then why not? Every other investment seems like it's gone to hell. Stocks and mutual funds have lost a third or more of their value. Oil and other commodities have collapsed by half. Real estate prices are down anywhere from 15 percent in Toronto to 30 percent in some Calgary neighbourhoods. How do any of us know if this is the bottom, or just a taste of what's to come? If this is a recession, then there's reason to believe we are close to the point where valuations have to start rebounding. But if we're not—if governments are unable to glue this financial system back together again with their billions in public money—does anyone know where the bottom is?

In a society built on debt, where the manufacturing base is evaporating, government finances are a mess, and job losses are mounting, the tipping point could be a lot closer than many people think—and than politicians and economists will admit. If consumers stop buying and few investors have the confidence to borrow for real estate, home prices could slide by half or two-thirds. That would trigger a wave of mortgage default and serious times for banks—even Canadian ones—who are already distressed.

In that scenario, it's not outside the realm of possibility a "bank holiday" could occur if enough people decide to bring cash home where they can keep an eye on it. Of course, such a thing would never be announced in advance. By the time you heard the corner bank was not going to be opening until further notice, it would be too late to protect yourself.

Meanwhile the non-performance of investment assets like stocks and mutual funds raises the serious question of where money is actually safe. Do you hand it over to an investment advisor and hope for the best? How about people—Baby Boomers—who are not exactly long-term, 30-year investors any more? Can you blame them for not wanting to see precious retirement savings evaporate?

And then there are those people (and I admit to these urges when I watch the financial news channel too much) who think we're way too close for comfort to a system breakdown. After all, what happens if governments run into a funding crisis, and can't keep the electric grid up and running 100 percent of the time? Without juice, this society collapses. No gas pumps. No ATMs. No online credit or debit card swiping at the grocery store. If you don't happen to have food, fuel, and cash when the lights go out, you're basically helpless. So, the easiest problem to solve, it seems, is money. In a safe. At home.

How to withdraw cash:

1. Withdrawals from bank machines are quick, but never think they're anonymous. All ATMs will record the transaction itself, including the denomination of the bills you walk away with, and most will also take a nice picture of you, which is fed online to the bank's security centre. You can wear a ski mask, but that might result in some unwanted police attention.

2. Bank machine cash withdrawals have daily limits, which are in place to help curtail bank fraud. So, getting at your life savings could require a lot of visits.

3. Be aware that taking large amounts of cash from a bank machine means doing this in a public place, which increases the chances you might be assaulted and robbed. Not smart.

4. So, large cash withdrawals are definitely best made in a branch. Try to choose a time of day when the customer count is down, to limit unwanted attention. Think like a felon.

5. If the withdrawal is over $3,000, call the branch before you visit and inform them of the transaction to come, and when you'll be there to get the funds. This will make the whole process go more quickly and attract less attention from employees and clients. They should also have the funds bundled.

6. In the bank ask that the funds be tabulated by putting them through the bank note counting machine, instead of being counted in front of you. The machine is deadly accurate, and you can easily read the LED display from many feet away, telling you the exact number of bills which have been

run though. The point of the visit is to have it last for as short a period of time as possible.

7. Consider travelling to a bank branch where you are not known. This will, of course, require that you show a valid driver's license or other valid ID, but it will help ensure the security of your action.

8. There is no limit on the amount of cash you can withdraw. At least, not yet. Limits are routinely put in place in other countries which have cash and banking problems, but right now Canada is not one of them. If this matters to you, why wait?

9. When it comes to the cash itself, make a decision on what denominations of bills will be of the greatest use to you. If the point is simply to convert a low-yielding savings account into physical money until the economy stabilizes and your confidence in the bank is restored, then large denominations are fine—hundreds or even thousands.

10 For most people, however, a cash reserve is best intended to finance your life in unexpected times—when the government declares a bank holiday, if there were a run on the banks making access difficult or if a widespread power outage closed the banks, along with shutting down banking machines, debt and credit card terminals, cash-back locations, and most (if not all) retailers. In that kind of circumstance, lower-value bills would clearly be preferable and more liquid. Therefore consider a stash of twenties, as well as a few thousand in fives and tens.

11. How much cash should you have on hand to deal with an emergency situation? A good rule of thumb is enough to cover your out-of-pocket expenses for six months. Those would include food, gasoline and diesel fuel, clothing, and emergency supplies, such as lanterns, kerosene, tools, portable generator, pet supplies, bottled water, and enough prescription medicines.

12. Don't try to hoard enough cash to make mortgage or loan payments. In the event of a financial emergency, those

could be the least of your worries. That's the bank's problem—let those guys figure it out.

13. When going to the bank, take an inconspicuous lockable briefcase or shoulder bag with you to transport the cash home. Obviously be aware of who is around you at the time of the transaction. Get a detailed receipt from the teller showing amount and time of withdrawal. Do not travel home on public transit or on foot.

14. Keep this to yourself.

WHY CASH IS KING

But is establishing a cash reserve at home, or another safe and private location, paranoid and excessive? Apparently the surge in safe sales shows that a growing legion of people don't think so, and yet this behaviour is sure making a lot of economists very nervous. More than anything else, that metal box with a lock on the front from Home Depot is coming to symbolize the most important battle we could be facing—inflation versus deflation.

The issue's simple. Cash is just as important to keep the economy going as it is to finance your own life. In a society where cash is taken out of circulation—even some of it—the effects can be immediate. "You're reducing the circular flow of income," is how US economist Cary Leahey puts it. "If you give your dollar to your plumber, your plumber can use it to pay a bill from his electrician. The electrician then goes to the grocery store, and that one dollar has turned over many times. If Homer and Marge decide not to go to the mall this weekend but put their money in a safe, you've got a problem. And it can be a very serious problem for the economy."

Of course, some would argue that this attitude—keeping consumers consuming, running up credit card debt, buying houses, or spending disposable income instead of saving it—is exactly part of how we got into this crisis in the first place. And they're right. Excessive credit and overspending is at the very heart of the collapse we are now dealing with, and which governments are fighting with their massive cash infusions. But economists also point out there's a difference between hoarding money in the bank, and doing so in the cold air return vent of your laundry room. Banks, after all, don't take your money and lock it away in a vault. Instead, they spend it to make more money—lending it out in the form of mortgages, credit cards, lines of credit, and business or consumer loan debts; all activities which make the economy work.

But those things also constitute risk. They're beyond your control. And they might endanger that bank if large numbers of people decide they can't afford to pay their mortgages any longer, or just to default on their credit card balances. Which, I hasten to add, has been exactly what's happening in the United States. That's a confidence-builder, right?

Nonetheless, if enough people storm the bank to retrieve their money, that action forces the bank to find the cash or to close its doors until it can. It also reduces the amount of cash in circulation—and that is precisely what's taking place. These days, both banks and consumers appear to be hoarding paper wealth. The amount of currency in circulation in Canada, the US, and Europe has been increased dramatically since the crash began—up to a level not seen in almost a decade, when we had that bogus Y2K * scare. And, as University of Western Ontario economist George Athanassakos makes clear, when there's a lot of money floating around but people don't want to spend it, or banks loan it, we get a credit crisis.

Without enough credit, everything slows down, sales stall, and corporate incomes take a hit. A good example was the feared collapse of the North American car business in 2008, as Ford and General Motors announced that because consumers were sitting on their money, those companies were burning through cash at the rate of two billion dollars a month each and were headed for that big wrecker's yard. Without a quick pickup in sales (unlikely) or a big injection of government money (almost certain), GM said would hit a liquidity wall and drop through the minimum amount necessary to operate its business. Cash, even if you're the world's biggest car company, is king. Without new cash from new sales, inventory builds up, production has to be slashed, workers are laid off, and prices fall to try to stem the slide.

This is exactly what is happening now, to car prices, house prices, flat screen TVs, and most other consumer goods. It's called deflation and it's the stuff depressions are made of. It's why we're all shopping at Walmart.

"Current conditions are consistent more with an increase in deflationary rather than inflationary pressures," Athanaasakos wrote in a *Globe and Mail* column. "The spectacular de-leveraging we have witnessed over the last few months has led to a buildup of deflationary forces, and this, over a short few months, has led to the collapse of commodities and gold prices and the prices of other investments that are considered good hedges against inflation."

> Major producers, like India and China, over-expanded capacity over the past 10 years and overproduced. The fear that all these products will be dumped onto world markets is reinforcing the expectation of lower prices down the road. Central banks around the world are trying to deal with deflation by flooding the system with liquidity, while at the same time guaranteeing bank loans and other investments, such as bank deposits, in an attempt to deal with the fear of default.
>
> Currently, in the battle between inflationary forces (too much money floating around) and deflationary forces (the unwillingness to lend/invest), the deflationary forces are winning in the economies around the world as the severe credit squeeze and de-leveraging that has been taking place are working their way through the system.

So, where do we go from here? Figuring that out is critical to making a personal decision about whether to yank money out of the bank in case you and your family need it in worse days to come, or be a boy scout and spend it all—maybe buy a new Chevy Malibu, or a cottage at fire sales price—in the hope that the economy will improve for all of us. If you are a cautious person, suspicious of the ability of central bankers and politicians to sort this out, then a cash reserve makes sense, as does paying down debt as ruthlessly as possible. If you believe as I do, that the forces of deflation have already been unleashed across the world and the years to come will bring still-lower car prices and tumbling real estate valuations, why not err on the side of caution? There may only be a 20 percent chance your bank will shut its doors, but is that a tolerable risk?

How to love a safe:

1. Determine what the threat is you want protection from—fire, flood or theft—then purchase accordingly.
2. A safe can cost less than $100 or as much as $7,000, but if your intention is to store a few thousand dollars in cash and prevent it being taken in a home burglary, there is no need to shell out more than $400, for example, for a wall-mounted unit.
3. Placement and concealment of the safe is just as important as its immobility and heft. The safest safe is one the bad guys cannot find.
4. The worst investment is a free-standing safe, especially one which lacks the ability to be bolted down permanently. Thieves can easily make off with a 700-pound steel behemoth and then crack it open in their own time.
5. One option is an in-floor safe, installed into the concrete floor of your garage or basement, then covered with a removable wood flooring or work bench. This is a permanent installation which you can do yourself with a rental electric jackhammer and concrete mixer, or have it done professionally. Floor safes can also be located between joists by

building a retaining form of wood or a basket with mesh wire lined with roofing paper and plastic to reduce condensation. Cement around the safe to the level of the floor.

6. An easier option is a do-it-yourself air vent safe, which fits inside the wall-mounted cold air return of your central heating system. Simply remove the existing grate, cut out the drywall or paneling at the back of the opening, insert the safe and screw into place. The advantage is a cheap price (under $300) and a completely concealed location. The disadvantage is that, if discovered, it's as easy to remove as it is to install.

7. A good wall safe can also be well hidden, and yet is more difficult to move if spotted. Most are built to mount between studs which are 16" apart, and attach to the studs with heavy screws or bolts. Pick a location inside a closet, behind clothes, heavy pieces of furniture, wall hangings, mirrors, bookcases, etc.

8. Look for a safe with both a key and combination lock, as well as a reversible door for versatility, concealed hinges, and live-locking bolts. No need to pay more than $300.

9. Consider a car safe, as well, for the transport of cash when you are changing locations, vacationing, etc. A compact, one-piece unit can fit under a car seat or out of sight in the trunk and is attached with a theft-resistant steel cable. Also makes sense for a boat or RV.

10. If you go to the bother of installing a home safe, then make use of it as a central storage place for birth certificates, passports, social security cards, spare credit cards, wills, and insurance documents—or anything else that would help in stealing your identity.

11. And gold bullion or coins.

Deflation is the opposite of inflation. When prices continuously rise—something most of us have been used to our entire lives—then it takes continuously more money to buy stuff. The value of assets rises, which makes the value of money fall. That's inflation. If your income does not also rise, you are a loser. But if you owe money in the form of a mortgage on a house which is gaining in value, you win. The asset value goes up, the debt stays the same, so your equity increases, and your ability to repay that loan is enhanced.

It was inflation on crack which hit the real estate market since 9/11. This hyper-inflation caused a bubble which drove the price of houses far beyond the ability of people to afford them, so it ultimately popped as demand dropped. This is the worst aspect of inflation—its ability to make the essentials of life unaffordable (though I'm not sure a media room and a hot tub qualify). In an inflationary world, savers lose and investors win. It makes no sense having suitcases full of cash sitting around, because its purchasing power is constantly eroded. You're far better off to convert cash into those things which are rising in value. And, finally, it makes great sense to borrow more money to do the same thing, since inflation pushes down the burden of debt as it increases commodity prices.

Take a mirror to all of this, and you have a deflationary world—the one we are entering now at a hell of a clip. In this environment, all the rules change.

Prices start dropping for commodities, then services, followed by business profits and wages. Lack of consumer demand forces prices below the cost of production, which leads to mounting unemployment, even less demand, and even lower prices.

In deflationary times like these, the value of cash rises and the cost of houses, cars, iPods, bank shares, pet food, and most everything else declines. That means purchasing power goes up for those people with money. At the same time, it makes debt intensely harder to pay since loans and lines of credit don't go down. With real estate, deflation is a double killer for two reasons: (a) house values drop below the price many people paid to get it and (b) because the mortgage debt remains constant its burden rises as equity is wiped out. This is exactly what's happened with scores of American families—more than seven million of them—who are in negative equity. There's no doubt the same is going to happen in Canada, as real estate continues to drop, turning homeownership into a nightmare for those who purchased a home since 2006. This is a disaster, of course, for people—like tens of thousands of autoworkers in southern Ontario—who have lost their jobs in this deflationary cycle, and yet live in areas where the cost of housing was high.

For economists, deflation is far scarier than inflation. It should be for you, too. This is what caused the Great Depression.

"Deflation is very scary, scarier than a recession," Standard & Poor's chief economist told CNN last October, "because once you get into it, it's harder to get out of." And this is exactly why governments all over the place have been pumping hundreds of billions into mortgage companies, banks, money markets, car companies, and insurers, and at the same time dropping interest rates as low as possible. They're doing everything they can think of to rekindle demand, spending and—yes—inflationary behaviour. It's what Barack Obama's stimulus packages are all about, since the guy has no desire to become the next Herbert Hoover. But can he avoid it?

Make no mistake about this: Governments want you to spend your cash and to borrow more money, which are exactly the two things which will destroy you if they don't pull this off and deflation rules. They do not want you to hoard money, take it out of the bank, install a safe or get all frugal.

Does this mean there will there be a depression? What is a depression? And what happened the last time there was one? Is it possible for a country to talk itself into an economic funk?

If so, we might be on the way. An online poll taken by CNN in late 2008 attracted almost 90,000 people answering the question of "How gloomy are you about the nation's economy?" Fifteen per cent said it wasn't so bad; 16 percent said it was bad, but they'd seen worse; and 68 percent replied this was the worst they had experienced.

But to actually have seen a worse economy, at least in terms of the stock market, car sales, real estate, consumer spending, or government financing, those CNN website surfers would have to have been at least 80, or more likely 90 years old. The crash of 2008 had taken an awesome and immediate toll on the US economy, which quickly ricocheted around the world. Banks and investment houses, insurance companies and ratings agencies were shaken to their foundations. Corporations lost business and profits evaporated, along with jobs. Governments borrowed new billions and saw their budgets shredded. Stock prices fell heavily, wrecking havoc on mutual funds, brokers, and Porsche dealers.

But that stuff doesn't cause depressions. It's not until households feel totally screwed over, stop spending, and cocoon that misery really sets in.

So, are we there yet? Is this just a really bad recession, likely to end within two years of beginning, or could this be the start to eight or nine years of grinding tough times?

RECESSION OR DEPRESSION?

Figure this one out right, and you might score, or avoid calamity.

If the downturn's going to be over sometime in 2010, with the stock market anticipating that fact in late 2009 and real estate rebounding six or eight months later, we could be staring a generational buying opportunity in the face. I mean, if this is a mere recession, how could it be otherwise? The Dow and the TSX lost about half their value in 2008 alone. Companies that had been trading at $100 a share were trying hard to hang in at twenty bucks by Christmas. Residential real estate listings exploded as prices sank, opening up—for the first time in eight or nine years—a massive buyer's market, in which investors with cash could prey on motivated, sometimes desperate, sellers.

That's the opportunity. Maybe.

On the other hand, if this mess following the financial crash devolves into deflation and global depression, loading up on bargain stocks and cheap real estate with either cash or money borrowed at bargain-basement rates could finish you off. After all, remember what happened to stock market investors back in the 1930s who were convinced the mess then was also temporary. History books are filled with stories of the 1929 crash, and most people have seen the famous "Wall St. lays an egg" headline from the next day. But the stock massacre of October 29 wasn't the end. It was the beginning.

The initial market collapse, lasting two months, shaved 47 percent off the value of the Dow (eerily similar to the 42 percent which vanished in September and October of 2008). Seven months later, stocks looked like they were making a comeback. Opportunistic investors poured back in, snapping up "quality" shares at prices they thought were ridiculously cheap. That's when the real crash started, a sickening descent which continued until hitting bottom in the summer of 1932. By that time the Dow Jones Industrials had lost almost 90 percent of their value. (It would not be until 1954 that the Dow matched its 1929 mark, meaning investors at the top had to wait 25 years just to get their money back.)

And if investors of the day were looking to the mainstream media and political leaders for credible financial news, well, guess what? They were had.

Why worry? Be happy!
January 21, 1930
"Definite signs that business and industry have turned the corner from the temporary period of emergency that followed deflation of the speculative market were seen today by

President Hoover. The President said the reports to the Cabinet showed the tide of employment had changed in the right direction."

— News dispatch from Washington

January 24, 1930

"Trade recovery now complete President told. Business survey conference reports industry has progressed by own power. No Stimulants Needed! Progress in all lines by the early spring forecast."

— *New York Herald Tribune*

March 8, 1930

"President Hoover predicted today that the worst effect of the crash upon unemployment will have been passed during the next sixty days."

— Washington dispatch

May 1, 1930

"While the crash only took place six months ago, I am convinced we have now passed the worst and with continued unity of effort we shall rapidly recover. There is one certainty of the future of a people of the resources, intelligence, and character of the people of the United States — that is, prosperity."

— President Herbert Hoover

June 29, 1930

"The worst is over without a doubt."

— James J. Davis, secretary of Labor

August 29, 1930

"American labor may now look to the future with confidence."

— James J. Davis

September 12, 1930

"We have hit bottom and are on the upswing."

— James J. Davis

October 16, 1930

"Looking to the future I see in the further acceleration of

science continuous jobs for our workers. Science will cure
unemployment."
— Charles M. Schwab

October 20, 1930
"President Hoover today designated Robert W. Lamont, secretary
of Commerce, as chairman of the President's special committee
on unemployment."
— Washington dispatch

October 21, 1930
"President Hoover has summoned Colonel Arthur Woods to help
place 2,500,000 persons back to work this winter."
— Washington dispatch

November 1930
"I see no reason why 1931 should not be an extremely good
year."
— Alfred P. Sloan, Jr., General Motors Co.

June 9, 1931
"The depression has ended."
— Dr. Julius Klein, assistant secretary of Commerce

August 12, 1931
"Henry Ford has shut down his Detroit automobile factories
almost completely. At least 75,000 men have been thrown out
of work."
— *The Nation*
(Source: Illuminati News)

As for residential real estate, it was pretty much the same
story. House values did not collapse with the stock market in
1929, but held reasonably stable, except for those folks whose
market losses necessitated bailing out (and only a sliver of the
population actually owned stocks). Most families stayed in their
homes, paid their mortgages, and carried on—until deflationary
pressures eliminated profits and jobs, while the bankers ended
their 1920s practice of making interest-only loans and severely

tightened credit. More than anything else, it was the explosive rise in unemployment—to a Depression high of 25 percent—which destroyed real estate values. By 1935 it was possible to buy homes for $1 (in 2008, by comparison, there were hundreds of homes for sale in Detroit on the market for less than $500).

The question, once again: recession or depression? Is this a time of unheralded opportunity, or the prelude to disaster?

On one hand, we have every government and central bank in the world, seemingly supported by the corporate media, trying to reinflate the global economy amid crashing interest rates and trillions in public bailouts. On the other, there are eroding house values, stock market collapses, plunging consumer sales, a credit crisis, and ballooning jobless numbers. No politician or establishment economist is talking depression, or even uttering the other d-word, deflation. But then, they didn't in 1930, either. The famous "sucker's rally" of that spring ended up destroying far more wealth than the initial market crash, and those folks who jumped in on the advice of, say, the President of the United States, ended up pretty much screwed.

Despite the ominous parallels between today and the months leading up to the Depression's icy grip, there are many who believe we are in little more than an economic valley and will soon find our way out. It's impossible, they say, for overall economic output to collapse the 10 percent necessary to qualify as a depression, or to get back to the point where a quarter of the population is without work. "If you define recession by GDP (gross domestic product), it could be over by the spring (of 2009)," UBS economist Maury Harris told CNN. "If you define it instead by the unemployment rate, which tells you a lot more about how people are feeling, you'll probably have to wait until the spring of 2010 for things to start improving."

The consensus of fifty economists polled by Blue Chip Economic Indicators was that we're all worrying about nothing. A recession in the US probably started in the summer of 2008, and will be history by the summer of 2009. That having been said, the establishment view continues, the unemployment rate will rise a couple of points, consumer spending will be very weak, and house prices will continue to decline another few points until government stimulus programs kick growth back into our lives.

Not so fast, say others. This may end up being "only" a recession, but it will not be a normal one—short and shallow—for a host of big reasons. As economist Phil Williams and others point out, these include:

- Consumer spending is maxed out. People are no longer able, or willing, to tap into their home equity to finance new purchases. The home-equity spending spree is over; credit card debt has ballooned as never before; debtor remorse has set in; and banks are sucking back credit as fast as they can as the whole financial industry hoards cash.
- Housing deflation and the bursting of the credit bubble will have a huge and lasting effect on the Baby Boomers, who were behind a lot of the excessive real estate-based spending after 9/11. Those Boomers, now staring at their sixties (as opposed to their psychedelic Sixties) have just lost a ton of home equity, plus seen their RRSPs, nest eggs, and 401Ks gutted in the stock market meltdown—a perfect storm, especially when combined with the increased chance they may soon be unemployed at an age when jobs are hard to find.
- Having had the crap scared out of them, consumers are likely to start saving again. In Canada, the savings rate has fallen to zero in recent years, while in the US, it's actually been negative by 2 percent, meaning households were spending 102 percent of their disposable income. Count on that to change. And the money which is stuffed into a bank account or a home safe or even a GIC is cash which is not finding its way into the coffers of companies through business loans, lines of credit, or the stock market. This will make any recovery slower as the pace of job creation snails along.

- There's not that much left to buy. In the three years or so prior to the crash of 2008, North American consumers went on an orgy of buying, loading up on the latest flat-screen TVs, iPhones, SUVs and crossovers, and computers, as well as unleashing a torrent of home renovation activity. The number of wrecks on the road has never been less, and our housing stock has never been better.

- Unemployment numbers could get a lot worse than most politicians and economists are admitting. After all, the real estate and construction businesses have been decimated. Wall Street and Bay Street have already been sending home tens of thousands of financial workers. The tourism and travel businesses are looking at lean years, and the slot machine palaces in Las Vegas and Windsor are already shedding workers. Next to be hit is the retail sector as sales tank, and meanwhile the North American economy has exported hundreds of thousands of other service and manufacturing jobs to China, India, and other low-wage countries. Finally, there is the auto business, where the Big Three all teetered on the edge of bankruptcy following the crash of 2008 with the near certainty that going forward there will be three no longer. These kinds of job losses could take years—not months—to reverse, even if investment and spending picked up instantly.

- And while the return on investments crashes thanks to ultra-low interest rates, while consumers are feeling tapped out and debt-heavy, the third strike is the steady erosion in house values which is making millions of people feel less wealthy. The demand for investment (rental) or recreational real estate has evaporated. Banks are once again looking for substantial down payments and proof of income to service mortgage debt—which guarantees less activity than the pre-crash days of zero down and easy credit. Besides, it looks like housing itself has more devaluation to come: 10 percent, or 20 percent or greater.

- Governments are also getting into the soup, along with corporations. Ottawa is almost certainly back into a deficit—

maybe a substantial one—just a decade after crawling out from under the last one. Ontario slipped into the red even as the first stock market crash was rolling through Bay Street. And in the States, the new president took office as the largest deficit in American history was being amassed. While the deficit spending and debt accumulation will continue, a point will come when politicians decide government services must also be cut.

• Pension tension. As large companies stagger and as stock markets devalue, the shortfall in funding billions in corporate pensions increases. Governments are responding by easing requirements to keep pension funds tanked up, but the fact that so many employee pensions are now potentially at risk just adds to stress and depresses spending further.

And there's one other factor at play here: China.

What clearly started as a real estate bubble and subprime crisis in the US is now anything but, even though housing values there continue to fall. The question now is whether or not the American contagion will lead to a global depression, by dragging down economies across the rest of the world.

Don't count on it, says Saxo Ban Group chief economist and Singapore-based Craig Russell. China has the power to stop all of that, as the world's third-biggest economy, which also happens to hold $2 trillion in US government securities. "Despite the bleak outlook for the US, consumer spending in China is rising," Russell writes for *AsiaOne*. "One can also argue that Chinese consumers have reached a mature age with aspirations and access to lifestyles similar to those of Japan, South Korea, or Singapore. Gone are the days when basic needs such as food and shelter were the priority. Demand has shifted to value-added items such as electronics, cars, and luxury items."

A more credible view is this: China's just going to make this whole episode longer and more painful. As the North American economy sputters into negative growth, imports tumble (especially to the US, where the dollar has soared in value since the crash of 2008) and major exporters like China feel the pinch immediately. Producers there slash prices and dump inventory in order to keep their factories open, and Walmart stores in Peoria and Halifax are only too happy to have the cheaper stock. Ultimately, though, this just helps erode manufacturing capacity on this continent, costing more jobs.

China, then, potentially becomes a giant agent of deflation. As its factories scale back, deflationary ripples are sent out to suppliers across the globe who sprang up to feed the emerging powerhouse. China has turned into a major importer of cotton from the US, for example, timber from Russia, oil from the Gulf states, and electronics parts from its Asian neighbours. Suddenly as the American consumer stops spending, China stops producing and the impact becomes more planetary.

Solid proof we're swimming in the same soup came in the final weeks of 2008, when China abruptly announced a $586 billion stimulus plan, as an attempt to stop the global financial crisis at its borders. Without warning, Beijing did all those things panicked capitalist governments were scrambling to accomplish—lower interest rates, a $17 billion tax cut for businesses and hundreds of billions into public infrastructure, railways, roads, airports as well as health and education, high technology, and affordable housing.

China's explosive 20 percent-per-year export growth could plunge to zero in 2009 and beyond, seriously cutting into the 11 percent annual rise in the economy. And while that may not sound like a problem in Canada or the US where growth will be negative, it's a disaster for the Chinese government trying to find jobs for the 15 million people who enter the workforce each year, who increasingly expect a middle class lifestyle and rising incomes.

"A small taste of exactly what the government wants to avoid came last month in the southern city of Dongguan, an exporting hub near Hong Kong," Reuters reported as the stimulus packaged was being unveiled:

About 1,000 labourers protested outside a toy factory, demanding unpaid wages after the firm, battered by the downturn overseas, closed its doors. In Wenzhou, an export powerhouse in the east, about 20 per cent of workers have lost their jobs, prompting an exodus to the countryside, local press recently reported."

Pain has spread throughout China, not just its export sector. Industrial production slumped in September to its weakest annual growth in six years, and real estate development has slowed as prices have faltered. Business managers have started to cut staff, a pair of recent surveys showed. Just last year, companies complained that China's surging economy had led to labour shortages and forced wages higher.

Communist or capitalist, what politicians around the world fear most right now is the same: economic collapse.

So there you have some arguments for this recession staying a recession. Governments everywhere are pulling out all the stops to stem the decline. Interest rates here are probably going to zero, or close to it. The price of everything, from stocks to houses to Escalades will continue to fall until buyers swarm back in. The financial system is being backstopped as never before with public money. Washington and Ottawa will simply not let a General Motors bite the dust. Our social safety net means even unemployed people continue to receive income and will stay consumers. Barack Obama's foreclosure moratorium will halt the real estate slide. We've learned too many lessons from the last depression to be dumb enough to walk into another one.

Really? But even if we've learned a lot, are the forces leading us to a far worse economy already unstoppable?

For example, in 1929 the bubble that ended up bursting and unleashing deflation was the stock market. But in the crash of 2008, stocks were hardly the only overvalued asset. In fact, financial market excesses were built on even larger bubbles, including real estate. "We entered the slowdown with massive overvaluation in all assets," says US economist Paul Kasriel, "commodities, stocks, mortgages and real estate." This, he maintains, will make dealing with and containing the fallout far more complicated and costly than in the years preceding the Dirty Thirties.

Hard to argue that. When the stock market crash of September 2008 unfolded, Canadians and Americans had already been battered around by the highest gasoline costs in history, the result of record-setting oil prices which hit $140 a barrel. That had already crashed car sales, especially SUVs, and led to GM's decision to lay off thousands of workers and shut its sprawling Oshawa, Ontario, truck plant. Already sales of Ford's sexy new Edge and Flex crossover vehicles were tanking, while truck manufacturers like Sterling and Navistar in southern Ontario were teetering. Already the value of houses in oil patch cities like Calgary and Edmonton had dropped and condo projects in Vancouver and Toronto were being cancelled. Already there were serious concerns in New York and Washington about the excesses of the derivatives market and the export around the world of toxic mortgages, as foreclosures around the country hit record levels and real estate values took the biggest hit since the Thirties.

Worse, in the 1930s North America's economy was mostly centred on manufacturing and farming—industries which could be primed by government. Today two-thirds of all economic activity comes from the consumer, and North America has turned into one giant, glorified, excessive mall—a service economy where we create wealth by selling each other non-essential products and services. As politicians have been discovering, it's a lot harder to restore consumer confidence than it is to subsidize agriculture, especially in the Internet age when fear and online panic can cross the globe in minutes.

But the main reason this may end up being more than a recession is one I've already mentioned repeatedly: Debt.

Hard to see how people will start buying houses again when millions of families are in negative equity, owing more on mortgages than they own in equity. Equally puzzling is when consumer spending will resume, with $900 billion in credit card debt outstanding and bankers tightening up on loans and lines of credit. And how can General Motors start hiring again, when its negative cash flow is $2 billion a month? Speaking of cars, when will we begin shopping for new ones, now that the car companies have stopped leasing? After all, household savings are non-existent, RRSPs have been chewed up by the markets and home values are falling.

Is all of this going to be repaired by the summer of 2010? And if it's not, doesn't that just increase the odds the downward spiral might intensify, as fewer companies manage to survive, more jobs are lost, consumer demand slips, stock markets fall further, global trade falls off, and the economy deflates?

So, yes, it is different now. This time it could be a global depression.

Would you be ready?

In a depression, 100 things to disappear first:

1. Generators (Good ones cost dearly. Gas storage, risky. Noisy . . . target of thieves; maintenance etc.)
2. Water filters, purifiers
3. Portable toilets
4. Seasoned firewood. Wood takes about 6 - 12 months to become dried, for home uses.
5. Lamp oil, wicks, lamps (First choice: Buy CLEAR oil. If scarce, stockpile ANY!)
6. Coleman fuel. Impossible to stockpile too much.
7. Guns, ammunition, pepper spray, knives, clubs, bats, and slingshots.
8. Hand-can openers, hand egg beaters, whisks.
9. Honey, syrups, white, brown sugar
10. Rice, beans, wheat
11. Vegetable oil (for cooking). Without it food burns, must be

boiled, etc.

12. Charcoal, lighter fluid. (Will become scarce suddenly.)
13. Water containers. (Urgent item to obtain.) Any size. HARD CLEAR PLASTIC ONLY. Note: food grade if for drinking.
14. Mini heater head (Propane). (Without this item, propane won't heat a room.)
15. Grain grinder (non-electric)
16. Propane cylinders (Urgent: definite shortages will occur.)
17. Survival Guide Book
18. Mantles: Aladdin, Coleman, etc. (Without this item, longer-term lighting is difficult.)
19. Baby supplies: diapers, formula, ointments, aspirin, etc.
20. Washboards, mop, bucket w/wringer (for laundry)
21. Cookstoves (Propane, Coleman & Kerosene)
22. Vitamins
23. Propane cylinder handle-holder. (Urgent: small canister use is dangerous without this item)
24. Feminine hygiene, haircare, and skin products
25. Thermal underwear (tops & bottoms)
26. Bow saws, axes and hatchets, wedges (also, honing oil)
27. Aluminum foil, regular and heavy duty (great cooking and barter item)
28. Gasoline containers (plastic and metal)
29. Garbage bags (Impossible to have too many)
30. Toilet paper, Kleenex, paper towels
31. Milk, powdered and condensed. (Shake liquid every 3 to 4 months.)
32. Garden seeds (non-hybrid) (A MUST)
33. Clothespins, line, hangers (A MUST)
34. Coleman's pump repair kit
35. Tuna fish (in oil)
36. Fire extinguishers (or large box of baking soda in every room)
37. First aid kits
38. Batteries (all sizes; buy ones with latest expiration dates)
39. Garlic, spices, and vinegar, baking supplies

40. Big dogs (and plenty of dog food)
41. Flour, yeast, and salt
42. Matches. ("Strike Anywhere" preferred. Boxed, wooden matches will go first.)
43. Writing paper, pads, pencils, solar calculators
44. Insulated ice chests (good for keeping items from freezing in wintertime.)
45. Workboots, belts, Levis & durable shirts
46. Flashlights, LIGHTSTICKS, and torches, "No. 76 Dietz" lanterns
47. Journals, diaries, and scrapbooks (jot down ideas, feelings, experience; historic times)
48. Garbage cans, plastic (great for storage, water, transporting, especially with wheels)
49. Men's hygiene: shampoo, toothbrush and paste, mouthwash, floss, nail clippers, etc.
50. Cast iron cookware (sturdy, efficient)
51. Fishing supplies, tools
52. Mosquito coils, repellent, sprays, creams
53. Duct tape
54. Tarps, stakes, twine, nails, rope, spikes
55. Candles
56. Laundry detergent (liquid)
57. Backpacks, duffel bags
58. Garden tools and supplies
59. Scissors, fabrics, and sewing supplies
60. Canned fruits, veggies, soups, stews, etc.
61. Bleach (plain, NOT scented: 4 to 6 percent sodium hypochlorite)
62. Canning supplies (jars, lids, wax)
63. Knives and sharpening tools: files, stones, steel
64. Bicycles, tires, tubes, pumps, chains, etc.
65. Sleeping bags and blankets, pillows, mats
66. Carbon monoxide alarm (battery powered)
67. Board games, cards, dice

68. d-con Rat poison, MOUSE PRUFE II, roach killer
69. Mousetraps, ant traps, and cockroach magnets
70. Paper plates, cups, utensils (stock up, folks)
71. Baby wipes, oils, waterless and antibacterial soap (saves a lot of water)
72. Rain gear, rubberized boots, etc.
73. Shaving supplies (razors and creams, talc, aftershave)
74. Hand pumps and siphons (for water and for fuels)
75. Soy sauce, vinegar, boullions, gravy, soupbase
76. Reading glasses
77. Chocolate, cocoa, Tang, punch (water enhancers)
78. "Survival-in-a-Can"
79. Woolen clothing, scarves, earmuffs, mittens
80. Boy Scout Handbook, also Leaders Catalog
81. Roll-on Window Insulation Kit (MANCO)
82. Graham crackers, saltines, pretzels, trail mix, jerky
83. Popcorn, peanut butter, nuts
84. Socks, underwear, t-shirts, etc. (extras)
85. Lumber (all types)
86. Wagons and carts (for transport to and from)
87. Cots and inflatable mattresses
88. Gloves: work, warming, gardening, etc.
89. Lantern hangers
90. Screen patches, glue, nails, screws, nuts and bolts
91. Teas
92. Coffee
93. Cigarettes
94. Wine, Liquors (for bribes, medicinal, etc.)
95. Paraffin wax
96. Glue, nails, nuts, bolts, screws, etc.
97. Chewing gum, candies
98. Atomizers (for cooling/bathing)
99. Hats and cotton neckerchiefs
100. Goats, chickens

(Source: The Power Hour)

From a Sarajevo War Survivor:

Experiencing horrible things that can happen in a war: death of parents and friends, hunger and malnutrition, endless freezing cold, fear, sniper attacks.

1. Stockpiling helps. But you never know how long trouble will last, so locate near renewable food sources.
2. Living near a well with a manual pump is like being in Eden.
3. After awhile, even gold can lose its luster. But there is no luxury in war quite like toilet paper. Its surplus value is greater than gold's.
4. If you had to go without one utility, lose electricity—it's the easiest to do without (unless you're in a very nice climate with no need for heat.)
5. Canned foods are awesome, especially if their contents are tasty without heating. One of the best things to stockpile is canned gravy—it makes a lot of the dry unappetizing things you find to eat in war somewhat edible. Only needs enough heat to "warm," not to cook. It's cheap too, especially if you buy it in bulk.
6. Bring some books—escapist ones like romance or mysteries become more valuable as the war continues. Sure, it's great to have a lot of survival guides, but you'll figure most of that out on your own anyway—trust me, you'll have a lot of time on your hands.
7. The feeling that you're human can fade pretty fast. I can't tell you how many people I knew who would have traded a much-needed meal for just a little bit of toothpaste, rouge, soap, or cologne. Not much point in fighting if you have to lose your humanity. These things are morale-builders like nothing else.
8. Slow burning candles and matches, matches, matches.

(Source: The Power Hour)

Of course, we don't need to contemplate hoarding water-proof matches, bulking up on canned gravy, or breaking into the neighbour's house to steal toilet paper to imagine how we'd cope in a depression, or a serious and unexpected economic downturn. Take Iceland, for example. That country's small but modern and progressive society was devastated and transformed in a matter of weeks in late 2008 because of the economic enemies identified above: debt and overspending.

The fall was stunning. Canadians should sit up and watch.

A 2007 United Nations report which measures life expectancy, income and education put Iceland at the top of the list among the best countries in the world in which to live. Per capita, this small country of just 300,000 people had the fourth-highest GDP anywhere, and unemployment was zero. In fact, Iceland's residential real estate building boom was responsible for workers being shipped into the country, especially to work on the acres of new homes being built in the capital, Reykjavik. All that changed in a flash, as a *New York Times* article described:

> Overnight, people lost their savings. Prices are soaring. Once-crowded restaurants are almost empty. Banks are rationing foreign currency, and companies are finding it dauntingly difficult to do business abroad. Inflation is at 16 percent and rising. People have stopped traveling overseas. The local currency, the krona, was 65 to the dollar a year ago; now it is 130. Companies are slashing salaries, reducing workers' hours and, in some instances, embarking on mass layoffs.
>
> "No country has ever crashed as quickly and as badly in peacetime," said Jon Danielsson, an economist with the London School of Economics.

Iceland was crunched in the global financial vice, its major banks socialized and the national government reduced to begging for international support. At the heart of the problem was a banking system which exceeded its capacity to manage risk, and got caught in the derivatives nightmare.

At the same time, in another modern, industrialized country with about the same population as Canada, things were sliding from worrisome to desperate. With little or no warning, the global economic contagion hit Spain, causing fears of Depression-era levels of unemployment of 20 percent, as a long economic boom abruptly ended. In one year, the country went from creating over a third of all new jobs in Europe to losing more than France, Britain, and Italy combined.

"During October, 193,000 people, or 6,214 a day, registered jobless in Spain, stretching dole lines around city blocks," Reuters reported. "Total unemployed reached a 12-year high of 2.8 million out of a workforce of just 20 million."

Could this happen in Canada?

You bet. And reassurances from federal politicians or industry leaders should not mislead you. Just days before the collapse in Iceland employees were being urged to continue investing in stock-purchase plans at their places of employment. Weeks later, not only were the jobs gone, but the stock people had bought—if it was in the "rock solid" banks—was worthless. In Canada during the 2008 autumn federal election, the prime minister said the country's financial system was strong, its banks impenetrable, and the government determined to have a balanced budget. Weeks later Ottawa announced it would be shovelling billions into the banking system and was itself heading for a deficit. About this time the Toronto Real Estate Board revealed that house prices had plunged 13 percent in a year and sales were down by a third. A survey of employers found hiring intentions had plunged.

"We're entering a really fierce global recession," says Kenneth Rogoff, former chief economist at the International Monetary Fund. "A significant financial crisis has been allowed to morph into a full-fledged global panic. It's a very dangerous situation. The danger is that instead of having a few bad years, we'll have another lost decade."

In Sao Paulo, Brazil, at an emergency meeting of G20 finance ministers and central bankers, Canada's Jim Flaherty was even more blunt. "This is a time of crisis," he told reporters. The contrast with his words of six days before the election were remarkable. "We're sure not going to run a deficit," he'd said then, smiling. "We will maintain a surplus in Canada and we will continue to pay down debt. We are a relative rock of stability."

So, if consumers, investors, homeowners, and employees are the last to know when a crisis builds, how are people expected to prepare, or to defend their families? The only answer to that is: Prepare now.

ARE THERE PARALLELS?

Given that we might not be able to trust establishment economists, the corporate media, or the elected for sufficient warning of collapse, what should citizens be looking for? As mentioned, if this is a recession, then buying opportunities will soon be at hand. If we're on the way into a deflationary vortex, then buying assets which may be worth half as much in four or five years is hardly a strategy. Remember that in deflationary times:

- Cash is king, and,
- Debt cripples. Mortgages, loans, and credit become far harder to repay.

In this world, commodity prices tumble and governments have a far harder time managing the economy.

Japan has some lessons here. After the explosive real estate bubble of the 1980s in that country, the Japanese went through more than a decade of steadily falling prices for both houses and consumer goods. Tokyo did everything possible, dropping the cost of borrowed money to zero and keeping it there—largely without result. If people or corporations don't feel confident about the future, they don't borrow, no matter how cheap it is.

Layoffs followed, which were excruciating in a society where employment was seen as a lifelong commitment by companies. That caused slumping consumer demand, and even lower prices—a vicious spiral typical of deflating economies. Sadly, Japan only started to emerge from this mess a few years ago, just in time to be whacked with the financial contagion washing eastward from a profligate North America.

Back to us, though. How can we possibly tell now if we're on the brink of worse times, or are we all just being spooked by events few have lived through before? Is talk of a neo-depression premature and gratuitously alarmist?

Yes, says the Conference Board of Canada, which issued a late 2008 report telling us all to chill. "Canada is expecting to skirt a recession in 2009," it said, "although the economy in general is slowing, it is still growing." The board also said while the US will be in negative growth until the end of 2009, recovery will follow. No depression. No disaster. Move along, folks.

And here's another best-case scenario, this one from James Galbraith, a senior scholar with Baird's Levy Economics Institute in the States, in an article published on AlterNet: "The government has the power and should use it, first of all to secure the liquidity of the banking system and the payment system, and then to resolve the underlying housing problem. These things should be done, can be done and if they are, the whole experience would be relatively mild. I mean, it'll be severe by the standards of the past 20 years, but it can be contained and resolved in the next two to three years." It will mean dislocation in the financial sector, Galbraith adds, "but no collapse."

Is this near-miss possible, or have we gone too far into an excessive, indebted society to get off so easily? After all, the last few years have brought that average house price of $750,000 in Vancouver, twenty-year-olds in the Alberta oil patch driving $70,000 luxury SUVs, and the creation of derivative-based financial instruments worth trillions that few humans understand. We've also borrowed more money as a society than any which came before, wired the planet up so we actually know what a group of architects in Iceland think when they all lose their jobs, and created a borderless, seamless planetary economy where dominoes can topple without interruption, affecting the daily lives of people from Kitchener to Kiev. Is it reasonable to think that just a slowing in the rate of economic growth is enough to restore balance and common sense?

Probably not. This is why it's prudent for everyone to be aware of the many parallels and comparisons which exist between today and two of the worst financial periods modern society has gone through, the Great Depression of 1929-1933, and the Panic of 1873. Times change, of course, and contrasts are never exact, but it might be folly on our part to think people in the past did not also get ahead of themselves financially, and end up paying for it. So here so some points to consider as you decide what your own financial strategy will be:

- By the depths if the Depression, 25 percent of workers were without jobs, financial assets had lost nine-tenths of their value, the American president shut the banks down for four days, home and farm foreclosures soared and people hated bankers so much that bank robbers Bonnie and Clyde were folk heroes.
- Today, unemployment is not even at half of those levels, but it is rising faster than any economist had predicted. In the one month the crash of 2008 was in full force—October of 2008—a quarter million jobs were eliminated in United States, bringing the one-year loss to 1.2 million. The impending collapse of the auto sector alone had the potential to triple that.
- The stock markets by the end of 2008 had not lost 90 percent of their value, but "only" half. Still, that amounted to the worst performance since the 1930s. The 2008 decline was roughly equal to the 1929 crash, which was soon followed by a second leg down, which was even more devastating.
- In 1929, relatively few people had direct exposure to stock market losses, and the lives of most citizens were not affected

until the results—tumbling profits and rising unemployment—washed over society. Today, however, there's a massive connect between the markets and the public. Stocks have become the cornerstone of retirement planning. For example in the US, two-thirds of all 401(k) plans—the equivalent of Canadian RRSPs—are invested in stocks, a percentage which had not changed in a decade. Thus, the recent crash had a devastating impact on the personal wealth of millions.

- In the 1920s, the stock market constituted the only financial bubble. In the time leading up to the 2008 crash, it was just one of several. Far bigger were bubbles in real estate, commodity prices, and financial derivatives. As such, a majority of people today have been directly and immediately impacted, compared to a minority then.

- In the 1920s real estate was undervalued relative to other periods, as measured by the Case-Shiller Index. Preceding the 2008 crash, it was grossly overvalued, and in dollar terms constituted the biggest financial bubble of all time. Concludes economist Krassimir Petrov, "The coming correction in real estate will be protracted and gut-wrenching, with an expected cumulative effect that is much worse than the Great Depression."

- As bad as things got in the 1930s, no countries went bankrupt and the bulk of the misery was contained to Canada and the US, with an impact in Britain and Germany (which helped spawn the Nazi era). Today significant countries such as Italy have public debt worth more than 100 percent of their economy, while major economies such as Pakistan (which also has nukes) have lined up for an IMF bailout.

- There were rough equivalents to subprime mortgages in the 1920s (like interest-only loans, and increasingly sloppy lending standards), but nothing like mortgage-backed securities, collateralized debt obligations, or credit-default swaps. These derivatives have created the greatest financial bubble of all time, based on residential mortgages of questionable quality and massively deflating real estate values. Worse, they were virtually opaque to regulators, media scrutiny, stock market investors, shareholders in companies that traded them, and the global community which is now dealing with their collapse.

- In the 1870s, US railroad capitalists also created complex financial instruments which sold well and gave a handsome rate of return—but, like securities derived from subprime mortgages—were based on nothing. When a European real estate bubble burst, demand for US products dropped, and interest rates rose, investors got a jolt. After railroad financier Jay Cooke was unable to pay his debts, the stock market crashed and hundreds of banks closed over the next three years. The panic lasted four years in the US, six years in Europe, and saw great numbers of people relieved of their wealth and property.

- In the 1920s there was no CNN, no websites. Fewer than 15 percent of households had radios and only one in five people read newspapers. The financial crisis took more than two years to spread from Wall Street to Main Street. This time, it took hours.

- In the 1920s the American dollar was a constant source of value, as was the gold bullion which backed it. Today there is nothing standing behind the greenback but confidence in the government. It is not possible to convert the US dollar, or the Canadian one, or any other currency into another commodity, the value of which is guaranteed by government. Alas, it's just paper.

- How does debt today compare with that in place when the Depression was ongoing? Far worse, actually. At the height of the last crisis the total amount of credit in the financial system reached a worrisome 250 percent of the GDP. Using the same measure, in 2008 the amount of credit surpassed 350 percent.

- In the 1920s, the 1870s, and other times of financial stress, it was clear who the sellers and buyers of financial assets were. But not today. Nobody now knows precisely how much debt is being held on what balance sheet, thanks to the trading in assets like credit-default swaps, which has led to a global loss of confidence, the freezing of essential loans between banks, and the need for governments to rush in with unprecedented amounts of public money to try and thaw credit. As economist Max Wolff interprets this: "We're dependent on our banks. Thus, the pain is ours. Millions will be fired. Retirements will be decimated. Opportunity will vanish, and consumption will fall. This will become more obvious and more painfully evident with each passing day. When it rains on the top of the hill, those who live on the bottom of the hill will drown ... The numbers about failures from car dealerships, stores and many small businesses are alarming and will get worse."

- In the 1920s there were no credit cards and consumer loans, not secured by real estate, were hard to come by. Therefore, household debt was minimal. It would be 1951 before Diner's Club invented the modern plastic card, which was designed at first to let just 200 of its most creditworthy customers charge meals at New York restaurants. Today the average American family carries more credit card debt than the average mortgage was in 1951. Unable to borrow more money against the plunging value of their homes, consumers have been using plastic to finance their lives. That's resulted in card debt approaching the $1 trillion mark and the growing number of payment delinquencies. As US financial analyst John Mauldin points out, over the last 20 years, consumer debt has risen to $2.6 trillion. Household debt, including mortgages, skyrocketed from 47 percent of personal income in 1959 to 117 percent in the fourth quarter of 2007; from 25 percent of GDP in the first quarter of 1952 to 98 percent.

So, in a nutshell, we have *over*-borrowed, *over*-spent, *over*-paid, *over*-mortgaged, *over*-invested, *over*-sold, and *under*-regulated our way into one hell of a financial mess. Our instant society has made the consequences immediate, painful, and overwhelming.

This has all invited the demon known as deflation into our lives, and resulted in these wholly unpleasant comparisons with the Great Depression and wretched past experiences.

It would be nice to chalk all this talk all up to journalistic hype and Entertainment Tonight-style pop excess. But this crisis is most real. As I said, at best it will lead us into a multi-year recession, reduced lifestyles, lost money, and jobs. At worse, we get to relive the past.

The recession Canadians now find themselves entering could become a deflationary spiral in the next year or so this way:

- If government's billions are unable to thaw credit enough to prevent a collapse in the financial system, triggered by that out-of-control derivatives market.
- If the stock market tanks in a second wave of collapse as it did following the sucker's rally of 1930. This becomes increasingly likely as more and more experts speculate that a market bottom is far below where we sat at the end of the 2008 crash. Some, like Elliott Wave theorists, are calling for the S&P index, near 900 as I write this, to drop to 50, while the Dow (now near 9,000) craters at the 400 mark.
- Or—if the world loses confidence in its benchmark currency—the US dollar. If Barack Obama stumbles, or fails to live up to the Herculean expectations, allowing the US to drop into a negative wage-price-earnings spiral.

Back to Canadian economist George Athanassakos, who offers this ray of hope: "In my opinion, the coordinated actions of the central banks and governments around the world will prevent this panic and credit problems from developing into a depression with its requisite deflationary consequences."

That's the good news. Then, he says, expect good old inflation: "But central banks and governments tend to overact based on past experience. When the credit problems are resolved, and banks and consumers start to feel more confident, all this accumulated (hoarded cash) liquidity and money supply surge may find their way back to financial and real assets, bid their prices up and in so doing take us back to square one, and a severe inflationary situation two to three years down the road."

Inflation. I miss it already.

And just in case Athanassakos is wrong...

How to prepare for a depression

There may not be one, if we're lucky. But then again, the stock market was not scheduled to crash, the housing market was not supposed to stall and then erode, and nobody six months ago expected governments would be rushing into debt and deficits so they could prop up banks, insurance companies, or the Big Three. Given what's happened in the past while, what guarantee do you have that a vicious cycle of unemployment and deflation aren't next? Right. None. So let's get to it.

Here are some prudent actions everybody should take while they can:

1. Pay down debt. Don't just resolve to do it next year, or start saving for it, or make an extra payment when you can. Be methodical and ruthless. List all of your debts with the interest rate charged and prioritize them for elimination. Credit card balances normally carry the most obscene charges, so get rid of that first. You are better off going to the bank and getting a consumer loan, then using that to clean off the cards. Obviously, stop using plastic. Go back to cash.
2. Don't cut your cards up. Just pay them off and put them away. If the economic crap hits the fan, you might just need an emergency cash lifeline.
3. Save money. Ten per cent of your income, no excuses. Just cut spending until you get there.
4. Renegotiate your mortgage, if you can. You are always better

to get a variable-rate home loan and now, more than ever. Interest rates are going in one direction—down. Also use one of the strategies in the next chapter to speed up repayment and save a mess of interest.

5. Start accumulating enough cash for emergency expenses. Six months' worth, no less. If you trust the government and the banks, stick it in a high-yield savings account. If you don't . . .

6. Get a safe and install it securely and privately at home. This is where the cash goes. And the paid-off credit cards. And the gold (see below).

7. Budget. If you do not have a monthly household budget, odds are you're spending too much money and simply can't account for it. Dude. Fix it. Establish a plan and stick to it because this is the only way you'll be able to save, accumulate cash, and systematically pay down debt.

8. Imagine you lost your job. Now live like it. Cut the expenses now that you probably would have to in that situation, and stop spending money on goods and services you can do without. Adjust your living standard down now, and if the unemployment freight train hits you in the coming months, you will already be partially adjusted.

9. Increase your income—by finding a part-time job ("Welcome to Walmart. Would you like a cart?"), or establishing a home-based or web-based business, or insisting your kids enter slavery and take on a paper route. By the way, try to retain your job—which could mean working extra hours for no additional pay, and generally sucking up whenever possible.

10. Don't panic and sell investments at a loss. The stock market may have taken a dive, and it might well be taking another one before this is over. But the odds are good it will recover, so if you don't need these funds, leave them be. However . . .

11. Get investment advice rather than trying to be a do-it-yourself investor. This is the time to spend a few hundred bucks on a good fee-for-service financial advisor or to scout out

an FA who is compensated through commission, and who comes well recommended. You need a steady hand on the investment tiller, not your own trembling fingers.

12 Don't panic, and try to come up with a family plan. If this does turn nasty, your kids must understand why the cable TV is being disconnected or those $300 running shoes are now off the agenda. Likewise, your spouse and you should establish reasonable, common approaches to lousy times and agree on the sacrifices and changes that might require—in advance. You do not need to be paying a divorce lawyer while you're worrying about Armageddon.

13. Educate yourself. Trust me, it helps. Know why we're in this financial mess and look for the indicators of where it might be headed—stock market results, retail results, employment numbers, real estate sales, and prices. Discuss these with your spouse, your family, co-workers, and friends. Financial difficulties can be incredibly insulating, so start breaking down some of those social barriers in advance.

14. Assess what you own. It's a good idea to create a list or database of all your assets, financial and otherwise. Not only will this help you keep a tab on your net worth, but it will also identify those things you might need to sell to raise cash in hard times. If the list includes art or antiques, don't get too excited—since these kind of assets plunge in value when the economy tanks. If you have a great painting you can live without, unload it now.

15. Establish a line of credit. No, really. Go to the bank and get the biggest unsecured line you possible can. You can never tell when you will need cash in a hurry, and so long as you don't access it, there should be little or no cost. It's cheap insurance against the unknown.

16. Reassess your real estate. More on this in a few pages, but before the Canadian housing market sinks into the swamp that's enveloped the American one (and it's coming, without a doubt) there is a still a chance to get your money out, to

downsize, to dump a recreational property, or to become a renter for a few years. This window of opportunity could very likely be gone soon.

17. If you feel better now, don't read the next list.

How to survive a depression

Getting caught in a total societal financial meltdown, with rampant unemployment, a breakdown of essential services, collapsed markets, worthless assets, rising crime, and economic despair is a bummer. Getting caught in one without having prepared is far worse.

Again, let's hope this never happens. But it could. And getting prepared is like buying life insurance or collision. You don't plan on cracking the car up or dying, but in the event those things do happen, you are better prepared for the outcome. Ditto for a depression.

Many will think the following list is extreme. Of course it is. A depression would be an extreme event, demanding an extreme reaction. In fact, a depression today would bear little resemblance to the one which took place in the 1930s. It would be worse, since eighty years ago North American society was coming off a largely agrarian existence when many people still maintained gardens and raised poultry, even within city limits. Most things were purchased with cash and everything functioned without any online component. Today our society is unbelievably more complex, which means a breakdown in any piece of it (like just-in-time delivery of food stocks to grocery stores), would ripple everywhere within days, or hours. Today virtually nothing works without electricity, phone communications or an Internet connection. In a protracted deflationary downturn, all would be under stress.

More importantly, most of us have lost all semblance of self-reliance. Woodstoves are rare, as are water wells and backyard vegetable patches. We buy almost everything with plastic, drive cars we cannot repair, and depend on government for the basics of life. In a modern depression, there's no guarantee this would continue.

So, in the range of options for the future, if a mild recession is on one end, disaster is on the other. Common sense and experience suggest we'll end up somewhere in the middle. But given what's happened in the last months, well, disaster may be closer than we all expected.

If you were to end up in a depression, I'd suggest this:

1. Get out of your mortgage. A true depression will sink residential real estate values by at least half and possible by three-quarters. If you bought a home in the last five years with financing on it, the chances of it falling below not only your purchase price but your mortgage amount are excellent. If that happens, you have no options. Walk away, and you'll get sued for the difference between the amount you owe and what the bank dumps your house for—and their lawyers never give up. If there is any chance you might lose your job in a depression and you don't own your home mortgage-free, you're rolling the dice by not selling now and getting out of this soon-to-be-crushing obligation.

2. Get out of town, or at least the big city. Take some of the real estate proceeds and buy a piece of land and maybe a used RV (lots of those for sale these days), and park it. Or move to a smaller, more remote community, where housing costs are far less and community support is far greater. If so . . .

3. Get a home with its own services, namely a well and a septic bed. If there is an economic collapse, don't count on governments to be there providing you with endless free, clean water, and the capacity to treat your sewage. All it will take is a sustained power disruption to end those niceties. And then what would you do? What will the millions who live in Toronto do?

4. Buy a generator. You can almost count on the grid going

down as utilities struggle with a declining revenue base and the cost of fuel to create electricity. If there is an ice or wind storm, it could be months, not hours or days, before service is restored as power companies struggle with their own financial problems and try to operate with reduced staffs.

5. Of course, for a generator, you will need fuel. A natural gas-powered residential unit will operate so long as the gas company keeps the pipes full (definitely longer than the wires overhead will stay up), and a propane generator can run for as long as your storage tank holds out (the company supplying you with gas will not be able to pump any into their vehicles without electricity). So a good bet is a large, well-installed gas generator and a few hundred litres of gasoline. Store it in 50-litre cans so it can be moved quickly if necessary and don't forget to keep a pump close by. You will not want to spill a drop.

6. Live somewhere you can plant a garden. Growing food in a depression is a no-brainer, giving you excellent nutrition at the right price. Get seeds now. Hoard them.

7. Get cash and store it safely. Covered above.

8. Get a weapon and learn to hunt. In the last Depression, deer and squirrels almost became extinct. Think about it.

9. If dining on rodent is not appealing, then this is another reason to move into a rural area. Chickens are easy to raise, and one of the most efficient machines on earth for converting feed into protein.

10. Change at least a portion of your savings into gold or silver, since these commodities are historic guardians of wealth. If things get really bad, Canadian dollars could become seriously devalued—a nasty lesson Icelanders learned in their recent brush with disaster. Precious metals are portable and universal, which is another reason you need that safe. Obviously, don't buy bars of the stuff, but rather gold coins and single wafers of one ounce to five ounces. Easier to pay for gasoline that way.

11. Make sure you have meds and first aid handy. If you or someone else in your home requires prescription medication, see your doctor and get what you need to fulfill a year's worth of it.

12. Buy and store food and water. Collect plastic bottles. Have a bad day box full of supplies—matches, wind-up or solar radio, lanterns and kerosene, camp stove and fuel, thermal blankets, tools including axe and hatchet, tape, pliers, the usual.

13. Get bicycles for your family. Sturdy ones with large tires. No need to pay more than a couple of hundred bucks apiece.

14. Get a dog. A real dog, like a German Shepherd or a Rottie. Although you now have to worry about dog food and caring for your pet's health, you have just secured the single best security device possible in a world which, I guarantee you, will be far less secure than this one. Besides, you get an extra friend.

15. Build community support. A protracted depression will tax everyone's ability to cope and there's no doubt you and everyone around you will need help. So find ways of helping each other. A communal garden could be far more productive than several individual ones, for example, with the constant care and security which will be required. Time can be spent in the evenings rotating between various homes, so precious generator fuel is not wasted lighting many houses separately. Find those on your street or in your building who have time on their hands, and can do the necessary maintenance and repair work that a condominium corporation or the city will surely abandon. Most importantly, find others to share your burdens with and to talk about sweeter times to come.

CHAPTER FOUR

A REAL ESTATE ARMAGEDDON

In 1995 I bought a newly-renovated 80-year-old two-storey brick house in Toronto's Leaside neighbourhood for just over $500,000. The area is centrally located, upper middle class and in demand. But garages are largely non-existent, as is privacy, and the lots are but 30 feet wide so our car's passenger door hit the neighbour's retaining wall every time Dorothy got out. In 1997 I sold it for $625,000 and felt smug indeed.

In 2007 the same house sold for $1.2 million, virtually unchanged from the day I'd purchased it from the renovator (who'd paid $325,000 earlier that year). In fact, just about every house on that street was in the same price range in late 2007 and early 2008. That meant the block was worth about $50 million. It also meant that to buy my old house with a decent 25 percent down payment would take $300,000 in cash, an income of $230,000, plus $40,200 for the land transfer tax.

There are lots of people with incomes like that, of course, but here's the question: Is an old house which cannot be expanded or improved, on a street of identical old houses built as a subdivision in the late 1930s, be worth a million dollars? More importantly, was a doubling of its value in a decade justified? Will it be changing hands for $2 million ten years from now?

Flash forward to the autumn of 2008, and house sales in Leaside were down almost 70 percent, but prices were off less than 10 percent—in fact many were higher—and despite pervasive news of economic mayhem, recession, and housing despair in the US. I spoke with my old agent, the guy who bought and sold that house for me years ago and is the realtor of choice there now. Listings, he said, were up by 300 percent and sales were down in that month by 85 percent. But of the 47 active listings in the neighbourhood, almost 30 were still on the market for more than a million dollars. "Many sellers that aren't in a must-sell situation are starting to pull their properties off the market," he said, "with the feeling they'll try again in the spring, hoping for some stability in the overall economy and less doom and gloom from the press."

And, he added, "Real buyers are few and far between, but there are lots of lookers, most with the attitude that prices will drop."

In this part of mid-town Toronto, where homes normally sold in hours, where buyers were in a queue for eight years for the chance to pounce on new listings, and where bidding wars were a usual course of doing business—a neighbourhood considered to be a bellwether of confidence by the aspiring middle classes—this was the picture he gave me:

2007 sales: 150

2008 sales: 42

And the snapshot is even more interesting when monthly sales are taken into consideration over the course of 2008, bearing in mind that the global financial situation started going to hell in September, and plunged into panic mode in October—despite deep interest rate cuts and government interventions aimed at restoring confidence. In Leaside anyway, it didn't work.

2008 Sales:			
January	8		
February	9		
March	13		
April	18		
May	15		
June	16		
July	11		
August	5		
September	8		
October	0		
Average sale price:	$1,023,606	Median price:	$902,503

Two hours to the south and west, a cottage on the north shore of Lake Erie came on the market for exactly twice what I'd paid for a similar property on the same road two years earlier. "What gives with these people," I asked Ray the local real estate guy, "don't they know what the market's like?"

And he said they wouldn't listen to him. "I've got 29 listings right now," he said, "all cottages—more than I've ever had before. Nobody's listening and the longer this goes on, the more it's going to hell." I asked him how many he'd sold in the past few months. "None."

A Coldwell Banker report published in late 2008 showed that three-quarters of its real estate agents surveyed said most sellers had unrealistic expectations of what their homes would fetch. Another study by US-based Zillow.com found half of the home-owners polled thought the price of their houses had stayed the same or increased in the last year. And this, of course, was a 12-month period in which the average home price in the US crashed by double digit amounts, for the third annual decline in a row and the worst rout since the 1930s. Said a Zillow spokeswoman, "It was very surprising to see this kind of disconnect."

Back in Toronto, the average selling price of a home tumbled by 15 percent in late 2008 compared with 2007, and by about 10 percent in the surrounding suburbs, taking the value down to just over $350,000, which was lower than it had been two years earlier. "That's a very big drop," TD Bank economist Millan Mulraine commented. "We expected things to moderate, but when you see double-digit declines like that, then the market is moving downward much faster than anticipated." And about this time, Merrill Lynch Canada's iconoclastic economist David Wolf was publishing a report warning that the "risk of an outright bust cannot be dismissed."

And Wolf is right. The declines witnessed in the course of 2007-8 are just the tip of an iceberg with the potential to punch a giant hole in the Canadian economy, given the fact most Canadian homeowners are trying to ignore an economic reality that has already decimated the American middle class. There is one inescapable conclusion: They will make it all worse.

Thirty-one hundred kilometres to the west sits one of the hottest real estate markets in the country. At least it was until the winter of 2008, when Kelowna started falling off a price cliff. At that time the average house peaked out at just under $550,000, and within six months had fallen by almost $70,000—a collapse rivalling that of US real estate epicentres Phoenix and Miami. The drop was an annualized 25 percent, or more than $10,000 a month.

But as with Leaside or the seaside, this was just a glimpse of what's to come. This is because so many of us have forgotten some basic House Rules which have guided residential real estate values for the last hundred years:

How to buy a house:

1. Never take on a mortgage with payments that eat up more than a third of your gross income.
2. Mortgage payments should not exceed 1/120th of the amount borrowed.
3. The monthly mortgage payment should be less than the rent being charged on a similar property.
4. What you pay for a house should equal between three and four times your annual family income.
5. The house should be affordable to the average family living in the area, or you will not sell it easily.

Using a variation of these rules, a poster to my real estate website, www.GreaterFool.ca, came to the conclusion that houses in Kelowna at the end of 2008 were bound to fall further—much further—losing at least 70 percent of their value:

Imagine that . . . a price drop of 70 percent. And this is a middle-of-the-road estimate; neither optimistic nor pessimistic. Now imagine if the world enters into a Greater Depression. If we do indeed end up facing harsh economic times down the road, we could easily see a peak-to-trough drop of up to 80 percent in the value of the average Kelowna home. Boggles the mind, doesn't it?

What makes these figures all the more realistic and rational is the state of the Kelowna and area economy. In a normal, healthy economy that can weather significant changes in prices, there tends to be 30 percent of the population employed in service-level and/or entry level jobs, 60 percent in middle-income, middle-wage jobs, and 10 percent employed in high-end, top-tier jobs that garner the highest wages. With this kind of a distribution, the middle-income, middle-wage families provide the economic buffer to moderate any bubble and cushion any crash.

Unfortunately, Kelowna has these percentages switched around—over 60 percent of our economy is service level and entry level jobs, many of which garner less than $12/hr (and this is in an economy where people require a minimum of $15/hr in order to properly support themselves, much less a family). Only about 30 percent of the jobs in Kelowna bring in a decent, middle-income wage. As such, Kelowna is particularly vulnerable to dramatic bubbles and catastrophic crashes.

As I have said countless times, when average folks in a community cannot afford the average house, prices will correct until they can. So when real estate speculation pushes values higher, buyers will resist unless they feel wealthy and confident enough take on the required debt load. This trip back to reality always happens. It can be smooth—a stagnant market in which sales slow and buyers find deals—or it can be a freefall, which has happened in some American markets and is about to happen in some Canadian cities.

The trip back to affordability is determined by how much of a detour the market was on. The forces of supply and demand have been pushed aside by two factors:

- Irresponsible lenders
- Greedy sellers

I covered some of the financing faults in previous pages. In the US, it was the subprime mortgage culture which destroyed real estate valuations by allowing them to bubble then burst. When prices rose beyond the ability of the market to keep growing on the backs of new buyers, mortgages became easy and cheap. Low introductory interest rates suckered borrowers who might be able to afford the payments now, but could never survive a future rate increase. Others who should not have been getting mortgages because of unstable, irregular, or deficient income were showered with money. Interest-only mortgages were offered to people who could not afford to pay back any of the principal each month. And no-money-down, 100 percent financing appealed to people (surprise!) who had no money.

By the start of 2009 it was estimated that, despite the damage already done, these excesses would result in foreclosures for an additional five to seven million American families by the end of 2010. And maybe a lot more, depending on the pace of job destruction. In response, Washington tried one desperate rescue package after another—by one account, 16 of them in 2008 alone. For example, in the last few days of the year Freddie and Fannie dropped interest rates to as low as 3 percent on several hundred thousand troubled mortgages, plus deferred some payments and set aside portions of the principle, to try and get payments down to just 38 percent of family income. Critics cried that was too little, too late, while others said asking folks to shell out almost four-tenths of their money for debt interest alone was obscene. At the same time, the cost of homeownership in Toronto was running at over 50 percent of income, and more than 70 percent in Vancouver. How could there be much doubt what was to come in Canada?

After all, when it came to bad financing, in this country we sinned just as badly. Zero down payments after 2005 became common everywhere. Even the big banks flogged mortgages to people who could not prove their income. And the introduction of 40-year amortizations allowed people to qualify for greater amounts of financing, allowing house values to rise. Worse, they ended up magnifying the debt load of every young couple who took one.

But those irresponsible lending practices just augmented the real culprit, which was house lust. So long as real estate values in Leaside continued to jump, enough people became infected to put down a million dollars for a glorified *pied à terre*. And as prices shot higher, the result made homeowners feel wealthier. Suddenly every $10,000 or $100,000 increase in neighbourhood house values became in their minds the base worth of their own home. Meanwhile higher prices meant greater concentration of wealth in one asset—real estate—since average family incomes were not rising. Houses grew more and more and more important to our financial lives, and as much a part of our identity as our jobs. Real estate porn was born.

The big difference between Canada and the States is that most Americans now regret they ever fell for the seductive charms and wicked ways of residential real estate. The roller coaster they've been on has stripped trillions of dollars of net worth from average families, cost millions of people their homes, damaged hundreds of thousands of credit ratings, and siphoned the retirement savings of an untold number of Boomers. And while some of them are still in denial, as mentioned above, the vast majority are not. They just want to know when the bleeding will stop. But, sadly, it won't be soon.

By contrast, Canadians—at least until the winter of 2008-9— had yet to admit their love affair was too tawdry to last. Prices came down only slightly relative to a big drop in sales because sellers had been resisting reality, as my old Leaside agent attested. The general feeling in this country has been that what happened to the US was an American phenomenon those Yankee subprimers somehow deserved. There was a belief, apparently based on nothing, that house prices here would dip a little—a couple more percentage points—and then go right back up to where they used to be. So, if you really don't need to sell, then don't. Just wait. It'll all be fine.

This is akin to stockholders in General Motors, who were appalled to see that industrial icon's shares dip to a 50-year low in the summer and refused to sell out cheap. By the fall, that stock was at a 62-year low and the company heading over a cliff. Some strategy.

Here is the likely scenario:

- The US real estate market will not even start to improve for a while, perhaps 2011, and,

- The Canadian market is running about two years behind that one. It will worsen dramatically.

As this happens we are all facing the same reality, which is continental deflation, a spiral down in prices and values, then jobs and wages, led by that one commodity we all thought was—unlike stocks or mutual funds—free of risk. The policymakers in Washington desperately trying to re-inflate housing prices know one thing well: the downward pull of the real estate market is the greatest economic threat capitalism has ever faced. And they are essentially helpless to stop it, since home values are destined to decline to the point where average people can once again afford them. Unspoken also is the fear among politicians that the housing experience will end up being so negative, so painful, that buyer confidence will not be restored now until prices over-correct, and families have tangible, irrefutable proof the danger of taking on mortgage debt is being erased by true economic growth.

When will that be?

Despite what the would-be sellers in Leaside think, stubbornly hanging on to their inflated million-dollar expectations, not any time soon. They know this well in Mountain House, California.

There are 42 million houses with mortgages on them in the US. At the beginning of 2009, almost a quarter of those—9.3 million—were occupied by people in negative equity, or about to get that way. That meant the value of their homes had fallen to the point where their loans were larger than the price they'd get if they sold. In some communities, like Mountain House—sixty miles east of San Francisco—negative equity became a community epidemic of disastrous proportions. In that town 90 percent of all homeowners owed more on mortgages at the end of 2008 than their homes were worth. More than 100 houses were seized by the banks in that year, many of them after the owners had left the keys in the kitchen drawer, packed up, and driven away.

And if you have visions of low-income families holding down

their belongings with bungee cords in the back of an old F150 pickup, think again.

Mountain House is to San Francisco what Oakville, Burlington, or Markham are to Toronto. The planned community was developed in 2003, a dream destination for upscale middle class folks who didn't mind making the commute into the city. Homes which sold a few years ago in the neighbourhood for $650,000 were worth as little as $340,000 by late 2008, and still depreciating. Scores were for sale. No buyers.

As the *New York Times* reported, 53-year-old Jerry Martinez bought in Mountain House in early 2005 for $630,000, and took one of the interest-only loans which have been commonly offered by both US and Canadian banks. The house was worth $420,000 three years later and Martinez joined his neighbours— who on average have negative equity of $122,000. Because his mortgage was structured as interest-only, the principal amount actually increased over time. But even if that were not the case, this family could not sell without bringing a cheque to the closing for at least $150,000.

But this is not just a tale of failed real estate or bad suburban investment decisions. Because most people in this area have seen their net worth sucked away by their houses, it's affected their entire economic outlook. The wealth effect that rising real estate gave millions of people has vanished. Consumer spending is down dramatically, which has resulted in the closing of most local stores and restaurants, boosting unemployment and helping create a vicious cycle which exacerbates the real estate decline. After all, who wants to move into a place where there are few services, where foreclosed and bank-owned houses sit for sale with little or no maintenance, and everyone is losing money on their investment?

Could this happen in Markham? In Surrey? Among those McMansions in the hills outside Calgary?

You bet. Count on it. Not identical results, but similar enough. As I mentioned, the Canadian real estate market is running behind that of the United States by about two years, and those with a mortgage who bought after 2005 need to be aware of the rising potential for negative equity. The first major urban newspaper to run a "negative equity" story may have been the *Toronto Star* in the final weeks of 2008. (A milestone event, after that paper's real estate advertisers banded together in the spring of 2008 to demand more positive coverage of their industry—notably after a review of my book had appeared in the real estate section. Shortly afterwards the section editor quietly resigned and ended up on overnight layout.) Slowly, the penny was dropping for media and homebuyers that no-money-down home purchases and long mortgage repayments were bound to yield sad results in anything other than a rising market.

"Mortgage broker John Cocomile says the current situation is fraught for those who bought with no money down. The concept 'is fine and dandy until the market goes soft.' You're in no position to weather downturns in the economy because you can't sell your home for cash, he points out. 'What if you lose your job?' "

Looking south, of course, it's been easy to see real estate deflation at work.

As *BusinessWeek* reported as 2008 ended, million-dollar homes across the US were becoming $500,000 houses:

> Art Tassario, a realtor with Friedberg Properties in the wealthy New York suburb of Cresskill, N.J., said buyers have all but disappeared in the past few months. Sellers who want their home to move quickly need to be aggressive about pricing. One method is to average the three lowest sales prices in a given neighbourhood during the past year and then discount that price by another 5 percent, he said. "If it was bad before, it's worse now," Tassaro said.
>
> Added a mortgage broker in San Bernardino County, California: "The only sales of million-dollar homes are foreclosures."

Back in the GTA and, more importantly, a year or two behind on the deflationary road, the *Star* reported on a couple in suburban Whitby—first-time thirtysomething homebuyers who had just purchased a 2,200-square-foot house for $315,000, with 5 percent down. After financing closing costs, they would end up with no equity. They were approved to borrow even more money than they did, "but they opted to stay in an affordable range.

"In spite of the rumblings in the real estate market," the story continued, the buyers were "calm" about their purchase, saying, "We feel quite good about where we are. In the long term, real estate is safe."

We have much to learn. We must understand deflation better, and follow the rules for coping with it.

As Canadian economist Mike "Mish" Shedlock points out, families are so indebted these days that no matter what Ottawa or Washington ends up doing, not much will change. Residential real estate is now beyond the ability of government to influence, since prices became so inflated and then were backfilled with so much debt. In fact, Shedlock says this all makes the deflationary situation we face right now a lot more dire than the one Japan struggled with for a decade after their 1990 real estate bust. That struggle, as I mentioned, lasted more than ten years—a sobering thought for anyone who thinks this thing will be over in a season or two.

Shedlock's conclusions:

- Unemployment will grow sharply higher—a trend which started with a vengeance after the crash in late 2008. Corporate profits took a dive, leading companies to slash expenses, and workers. This will be more significant in North America than it was in Japan, where employees enjoy more loyalty and respect from the boss.
- Much consumer debt—mortgages, credit cards, lines of credit, student debt—can't be repaid and will be defaulted on. This will increase as unemployment mounts.

- The housing market will continue to contract. Why would it not?

- The debt burden will be very unequal. Those least able to carry it through an economic downturn will struggle with the greatest mortgages. This group contains far more GenXers than it does Baby Boomers. Another reason to hate us.

Says Shedlock: "The pent-up deflationary forces are such that Deflation American Style figures to be far worse than Deflation Japanese Style. Here is one similarity: fiscal stimulus failed in Japan. Fiscal stimulus is doomed to fail in the US. The consequences for the US will be severe."

Would that mean government bailouts of more than $1 trillion in the US and $75 billion in Canada (by the end of 2008) are for nothing? Or was the point to keep deflation from becoming depression?

Does this gloomy outlook hold equally true for Canada? That was the conclusion I reached early in 2008 when researching for the book, *Greater Fool*. In subsequent weeks I forecast that Canadian real estate prices would fall over coming months by between 15 percent and 40 percent depending on the market, with the greatest declines in the West, where Vancouver was hyper-inflated, and with Alberta destined to run headlong into falling oil prices. Toronto, thanks to a large population and a more diversified economy, would see less damage. Sadly, I was correct. By November of 2008, the Canadian Real Estate Association itself was reporting a 14 percent plunge in year-over-year sales—the worst drop in 14 years. "The breadth and depth of the drop in activity suggests a major downshift in consumer psychology," said CREA economist George Klump, a former staunch denier of any cracks in the nation's housing foundation. More darkly, BMO economist Doug Porter added, "These figures on the surface would suggest the bust has begun."

Indeed. In fact, now I also understand that I was far too conservative months earlier. Nor could anyone see back in January the magnitude of the crash which would sweep through financial markets in September and October.

The reasons for most people not to buy residential real estate (at any price) are mounting. I'd have a hard time recommending taking on debt to get a house in the next two years. For the cautious, better a five-year wait. But if you do decide to buy in coming months, be prepared to lose capital. Here's why:

Ten reasons house prices will continue to fall

1. Jobs are being destroyed in the post-crash shock that corporations are feeling. The pace of unemployment will be relentless in the coming two years, driving down the economy, consumer spending, and borrowing. The number of potential homebuyers will dwindle and as supply of homes for sale overwhelms demand, and prices will continue to slide.

2. Government bailouts will fail to re-inflate the economy of the US, Canada, Europe, or China. As stock markets see clear evidence that there is no magic bullet, another wave of selling could occur (reminiscent of what happened in the summer of 1930), which will shatter popular confidence and stall any real estate recovery.

3. It is much cheaper to rent a home than to buy one, so until there is a powerful incentive to own real estate (like a sure-thing capital gain) there's no reason to expect prices to rise. Anyone looking to improve their family's finances will conclude that tenants win in this environment.

4. Real estate cannot rise in value without a steady diet of new buyers, and right now potential first-time purchasers have been shut out of the market by a return to more traditional financing. With the end of zero-down payments and 40-year amortizations in Canada and the collapse of the sub-prime lending market in the US, it takes actual money to buy a house. New buyers will have to save for a down payment—and that takes years.

5. Interest rates may have been forced down by central banks, but that didn't make mortgages much cheaper. The credit crunch has tightened up on lending terms and rates, just when buyers were thinning out. Bad news for the market.

6. Armies of small-time housing speculators have been caught and crushed in the real estate meltdown. In Toronto alone it was estimated in 2008 that 30 percent of all the new condos under development (more than 50,000) had been purchased by flippers, usually for minimal cash and with maximum financing. These people will either walk away from their investments before closing, rent them out for whatever they can get to offset monthly losses, or dump them on the market at fire sale prices. The dampening impact on the market as a whole—prices in particular—should not be underestimated. The last time something similar happened, in the early 1990s, condo values plunged by 40 percent.

7. Plunging financial markets and plopping house values are hitting the soon-to-be-retired Boomers especially hard. These people had been drivers of the real estate market for decades and have a huge amount of net worth tied up in their homes. Their exit as buyers from the market is a downer for everybody, and the certainty that they'll be desperately dumping properties in the coming few years will further crash values.

8. Builders and developers are in a vice. Sitting on acres and acres of development land or half-built towers, with millions in bank financing hanging over them, many will be forced to dump inventory at any price. The result will be predictable, and many simply will not survive.

9. As energy costs rise and disposable income falls, a large amount of housing stock will simply be unsalable. Suburbs will fall out of favour, areas without light rail transit or reliable bus transit will suffer more price depreciation, as will homes that are not energy efficient. Price deflation may be our future, but it will be combined with energy inflation.

> 10. Houses are not cheap enough yet for people to afford them. The basic reason this bubble burst is the most pervasive and powerful. Until the average family can live in a property of their peers, having put 20 percent of its price down in cash and able to finance the remainder on a third of their income, prices will continue to soften.

Remember that going forward, residential real estate has four strikes against it:

- *Price*: It took the market eight years to inflate, and it may take just as long to deflate. How can anyone expect that a 15 percent dump in Toronto or Calgary prices can balance out prices which doubled in many areas between 2004 and 2007?
- *Affordability*: No matter what the dollar cost of a property is, the key factor is the ability of a buyer to afford it. When unemployment goes up, affordability goes down. This recession (or whatever it ends up being) will be with us for a few years. Millions of families will require a long time to pay down the debt they walked into so casually during the bubble years. Going forward, they'll be cautious about making the same mistake again. This is a key reason housing prices could stay dramatically lower for much longer than most experts (and all realtors) expect.
- *Demographics*: The downward drag imposed on real estate by the Boomers is just getting started. When these folks understand their RRSPs and 401(K)s are not going to rebound fast after the crash, they'll be trying to unload houses. For all of us, this is uncharted territory. For the first time in Canadian history we will experience a third of the entire population hitting retirement age more or less simultaneously.
- *Energy*: Oil prices may have crashed along with stock values in 2008-9 (and will be rising again in the inflationary times to come), but energy consciousness is here to stay. That has

changed real estate tastes, and will continue to do so. This is why natural gas-sucking five-bedroom McMansions with hot tubs and three car garages are so, so 2006. The years are at hand when people will need to worry not only about their job security, but also weather events and food. Climate change and energy can take a back seat to economic distress for a while, but eventually the impact of peak oil, food inflation, stable power sources, and environmental refugees into Canada will seize us.

In total, we have a perfect storm blowing down house prices. A battered real estate sector in turn becomes a massive anchor on economic growth. It erodes family wealth. It makes us feel poorer. It collapses discretionary consumer spending—bad news in an economy which is more than 60 percent dependent on people shopping.

But it's only started—important news for anyone who's been thinking of selling.

By the time this deflationary bear market in real estate is over, we'll see that it came in two waves. The first started in the US with the popping of the housing bubble in the beginning months of 2006, and was followed in the spring of 2008 in Canada by a dramatic decrease in sales, leading to a gradual but steady slide in prices. The second wave came in the States with the explosion of negative equity and corporate layoffs that followed the stock market crash of 2008, and in Canada is likely to begin at the end of 2009 or the spring of 2010 as we all understand there is nothing unique about the country, and no northern antidote for housing contagion.

"The end of the decline in home prices will come only when there are no new economic forces driving them down," US financial commentator Martin Weiss says. "When will that be? I'd love to say it's just around the corner. But everything I see tells me that, despite the sharp declines already recorded, a steeper plunge in home values is dead ahead. The reason: So far most of the troubles in the housing market have been caused by bad mortgages going sour. Meanwhile the more common causes of housing slumps—high interest rates, rising unemployment and recession—are just starting to kick in. And the most powerful causes—depression and deflation—are still on the horizon." While it is unclear if a depression is in our future, there can be little doubt that deflation is. In fact, it arrived shortly after the crash.

Below are the approximate price reductions from the peak to the trough which will have taken place in both countries by the time the housing market is finally re-inflated by a torrent of pent-up demand:

	First Wave	Second Wave
United States:	17 percent	40-55 percent
Canada:	15 percent	35 -50 percent

These final numbers will undoubtedly be controversial, with the real estate community in Canada scoffing at the possibility that an Edmonton home which sold for $400,000 in 2007 could be changing hands in 2010 for $160,000 less. But chances are I may be too conservative in my estimates, should recession become the deflationary episode we loosely term a depression. The odds of that happening grow daily.

This is not good news for those clients of my old real estate agent in Leaside, who in the final weeks of 2008 were pulling their expensive homes off the market, hoping to score better deals in the spring. Bad move. They would have been far better off to just drop the prices until a buyer was found—even if that reduced a million dollar home to $850,000 or less. After all, a 15 percent haircut is better than one of 40 percent.

And that brings us to the key topic of selling.

If this is you, it's time to sell

- If you're a homeowner concerned about your financial future, with the bulk of your net worth tied up in your house (like most people), then you should sell immediately. There are more losses coming.
- If you cannot afford to see the value of your property cut by a third or a half, sell.
- If you have a mortgage equal to 75 percent or more of your current appraised value, I suggest you consider selling.
- If you bought a home with little or nothing down, your chances of being in negative equity over the next year or two are very high. You must decide if you will hang on to the home until your equity is restored—which might well take five years—or sell now and walk away with little, or nothing, and rent. Panicking and selling a year from now could result in a substantial loss.
- If you have trouble coping psychologically with the idea that your home will steadily erode in value, then get out now.
- If you've been holding out for a market recovery in the next season or two, realize it could be a very long time before prices rise to match your expectations. After Toronto houses topped out in the bubble of the late eighties, it took 13 years for the average home value to regain the peak. In Calgary the oil price-induced housing market correction of the mid-eighties took two decades to recover. A similar experience today—in the wake of a far larger run-up in house values—could put that Leaside house back in the million dollar range in the early 2020s. In Calgary, well, peak oil means peak house.

Studies show most of us have a far harder time coping with real estate losses than we do with reversals on financial investments, especially when that property is our home. "The reason, I believe, the effects are smaller for financial wealth than for housing wealth is that people tend to view those changes in housing wealth as more permanent," according to California economist Gary Painter. "Consumption will be impacted by the decline in housing wealth for a while."

In fact, the estimate is that housing value decline already seen by the end of 2008 would shave at least another $105 billion off the US economy the following year. That was a hundred billion dollars that wouldn't flow through corporations, leading inevitably to more layoffs and—as you might imagine—a more stagnant real estate market.

The second wave of the decline in both the US and Canada will be the result of the same thing—joblessness, since there's no one other factor which has an equal impact on affordability and consumer confidence. And evidence mounts that this may not be a temporary shift in global fortunes. With the United States running a trillion dollar deficit (that's a thousand times a billion, or $1,000,000,000,000) in the first year of the Obama era, and with the national debt exceeding ten times that amount, the final days of American global economic dominance seem to be upon us.

With China and India seeing growth rates five or six times that of North America, with their combined population base of 2.5 billion, with the emergence there of a voracious new middle class, an explosive entrepreneurial spirit, and an unfettered desire to succeed—as witnessed by the stunning perfection of the 2008 Beijing Olympics—global economic power is shifting from West to East. The sheer excesses of the American real estate market, surpassed only by the greed of Wall Street in flogging toxic mortgages and the abrogation of oversight by Washington in allowing it all to happen, have seriously tarnished America. Its investment banking industry has been wiped out, its public finances hollowed and the symbols of its industrial might—such as General Motors—are now emblematic of failure. Time for this giant to be reinvented. And it will happen, bringing new opportunity. In the meantime, though, the tigers of the East will gladly grab the reins of influence, directing a lot of investment capital from here, to Chindia.

This is why your house will be worth less than it was when you lived in, or beside, the greatest economy in the world. Going forward it'll be worth what one of your neighbours wants to pay for it. More importantly, what she can afford to pay. Imagine that.

This return to real estate fundamentals is hugely significant.

- It should coax family wealth out of houses, whose value will remain flat, and divert this money into financial assets. That's good for the stock market, good for the economy. Good for household net worth, too, since it brings diversification. Having more than 80 percent of family wealth in just one asset—the house—was akin to gambling your future on the value of one stock or mutual fund.
- It will dampen speculation, which does almost nothing to create jobs and build companies. Bubbles of any kind, whether in houses, tulips, gold, oil, or bauxite, are destructive because they divert attention, and always end badly.
- It will dampen our descent into debt, as we all learn again that mortgages exist to be paid off, not as a tool to accomplish effortless capital gains.
- This will end up being extremely bullish and positive for financial assets and knock down the price of real assets. After hitting its bottom in the second wave of selling after the crash of 2008, the stock market will be the focus of investor attention for several years to come, for the reasons mentioned above. Energy insecurity, climate change, demographics, and debt are all deflators of real estate. But the innovation and technology needed to deal with energy and the environmental challenge, to reinvent transportation, take us further online, harness new forms of power, and spawn vital new green industries in North America will be the new catalyst for growth.

The consumer-driven service economy, where we all sell each other houses for more and more money is dying. Those who realize this now still have a chance of getting out before the second and more devastating wave of selling and deflation hits the residential real estate market. Don't wait for the next, better selling season to come. It won't.

HOW TO SELL IN A FALLING MARKET

If you fall into one of the categories listed, I strongly recommend you bail. On the other hand, if you live where you're happy and secure, if you own your home debt-free or with a manageable mortgage, if owning has stabilized your housing costs in an uncertain world, and if you just don't care if your house loses half its value by the time this storm is over, then ignore the following strategies. Real estate is going back to its primary role as shelter. The Monopoly game's over.

But how do you unload your real estate to escape from debt or to liberate the wealth you need to live on, or to invest in next year's rapidly rising financial assets, in a horrible market? This will take determination and realism since sellers now and in the year or two ahead will face a huge amount of competition. As there will be a second wave of price reductions, so will there be a second flood of listings, as hundreds of thousands of families realize a better time to sell is not coming. Among those listings will be scores of those Boomer houses—larger, multi-bedroom, older (1970-90) dwellings—stuck on the market years too late by people who were not paying attention.

Remember a hard and fast rule: real estate deflation first attacks the places where most money sits. As I mentioned in *Greater Fool*, this is exactly why every city in North America has rows of stately 19th Century and early 20th Century mansions sitting in some of the worst parts of town. As harder times moved in, these properties proved unsalable as single-family residences and were eventually converted into flats, apartments, and tenements. As the market for luxury housing evaporated, driven down by lost fortunes, higher maintenance costs, changing tastes, and a shift of money out of bricks and mortar and into securities, they were carved up. Every time I drive down Jarvis Street in Toronto, I am reminded of this. What was millionaires' row a century ago, lined with hulking brick and stone family fortresses surrounded by iron fences, became the definition of seedy and downscale before finding rebirth in the recent condomania.

The Boomers' greatest investment mistake—buying the wrong kind of real estate, then dumping it at the wrong moment—will help drag suburban values lower. This will be especially true as oil prices rebound from the commodity price crash and the energy crisis is once again upon us all. But unlike the big houses of the past, today's suburban excesses are wholly unsuited for conversion into anything. Building standards have fallen and materials have become flimsy. In fact, many homes just 20 years old are near the end of their useful lives, with particle board subfloors, single brick exterior walls, and endless lengths of leaky, dusty interior ducts. Conversion into income-generating properties is also nixed by local governments who—at least for now—cling to a dying myth that single-family homes attract a better class of people than rental housing. That will surely change.

So, the 'burbs are dying. Got a house outside the city? Get it listed now.

Selling strategies in a tough market

- Don't cheap out and try to sell a property on your own, privately. You won't stand a chance given the array of competition you face. There is no option but to get on MLS (the Multiple Listing Service), and to do that, you need a realtor. Suck it up and find one.
- Shop around for that person. Visit houses in your area that have sold and ask the people living there who listed their property, who brought in the offer, and what kind of experience they had. Drive around and see who's got the most

listings in your area, and what's moving. List locally, not with a person from the next city or neighbourhood, even if they're related to you. In a cold market, you need an aggressive and experienced person who's been through an environment like this before. Not surprisingly, relatively few have.

- Interview a few agents. Ask them for two things: A marketing plan and a suggested listing price. The first is way more important than the second.
- But the asking price is critical. If it's abnormally low, questions can be raised about what's wrong with your house. If it's too high, buyers will simply pass you by—and this is the greater problem. Overpriced homes typically sit on the market and get stale. By the time the inevitable price reduction goes through there's no excitement generated by the listing, which means more reductions will be necessary before the house finds a buyer—quite possibly at a significantly lower price than you expected or needed to settle for. So, get it right the first time.
- This is where agent experience counts. You're usually better off not choosing the guy who gives you the highest number, since I guarantee he'll be back looking for a reduction after a few weeks—when your best marketing time has been used up. Instead, work with a person who knows the area, and can provide you with all the comparables. Then come up with a realistic value and knock a few thousand (or tens of thousands) off that. Trust me, you want a quick sale. Lassie's dying here.
- Don't get bent out of shape over the sales commission, either. The traditional 6 percent levy is toast now that the market has turned, so you should get a good person for a point or two less (perhaps more). But understand the less money in the deal for the agent will translate into a weaker marketing effort for your house. In a competitive time, you need someone who will advertise and promote as widely as possible. That's why you want a marketing plan in your hand before you sign the listing agreement.

- Once you list, hold up your end of the bargain. The house needs to be 100 percent at all times, ready for a showing on a moment's notice. Never insist on 24 hours' notice. In fact, never require any notice at all, other than a phone call. When there are hundreds or thousands of properties to choose from, potential buyers will simply move on to the next house if they can't get into yours when they feel like it. Doing your part means the house is perfect, by the way. No pizza cartons in the kitchen. No half-rebuilt truck engines in the garage. No *Debbie Does Dallas* videos in the media room. No mobile surprises in the basement.

- Be completely prepared for the questions a potential buyer will ask. Have a survey available, along with utility bills for the past year, and a history of your property taxes. It's always a good idea to sit down and write a feature sheet describing the neighbourhood's attributes, like schools and transit routes.

- In fact, when you're up against competing listings in your 'hood, probably on your own street, you need an advantage. Like staging. Most cities have staging companies which will come and advise you on how to improve the look of your houses by eliminating clutter, changing colours, shifting furniture or (more likely) getting rid of a bunch of it. Better still, invest a few bucks and let them move in and redo the place, renting appropriate furniture, painting some walls, and giving buyers a sense that the place is completely ready for their presence. My friend and employee did this for a suburban home she and her husband had been in for 27 years. It was filled with stuff that had sentimental meaning but did nothing but clutter up the place and obscure its better features. She sold recently, and quickly, and got her price even when three other houses were available on the same block.

- Don't be shy about spending some money to improve your chances of snaring an offer. The most cost-effective investment anyone can make is in paint. Inside the house, make small spaces look bigger with whites and neutral tones, while you can add a more intimate and human scale to giant Eighties family rooms or those awful two-storey foyers with darker colours. Outside, a paint job is a must, since gleaming trimwork will suggest that everything else is in great shape, even it is isn't. Curb appeal still sells houses. Never forget it—so make sure every inch of the trip from the car to the front door is perfection.

- Nine of every ten buyers these days goes online and researches homes to view. So, review what your agent plans to do with his or her website, and ask to see what photos will be loaded onto mls.ca, plus the word description. For a small cost you can also set up your own website under your address, like 487MapleAve.ca, and load it with all kinds of photos, a feature sheet, comments on the neighbourhood, and reasons you have enjoyed living there and are distraught to leave. Email the link to every person you can think of, and ensure it's a prominent element of your agent's site, as well as posted with your listing on mls.ca.

- When you do get an offer, be as flexible as possible and try to keep it alive. The longer the two parties go back and forth, the better the odds a deal will eventually be struck. Expect to be low-balled, of course. In this kind of market, that's a given. So, don't be miffed, piqued, vexed, or flummoxed. Instead, sign it back for what you can live with, recognizing full well that if you look greedy or inflexible, there are many more sellers out there who would love to have any offer at all. That's why they call this a buyer's market. Get used to it.

- Chances are the offer will also be stuffed with conditions, since they're all for the protection of the buyer, who is in the driver's seat. The offer might be conditional on the purchaser finding financing (not an unreasonable request if you give just a few days to have it removed), or on selling another home (not good). More certain is that you'll have to provide a survey, warranty that appliances and mechanicals are in good working order at the time of closing or agree to a satisfactory home inspection. This is almost always carried out at the buyer's expense, although I've seen some cheapos try to foist that on the seller. The offer could also stipulate that you include all appliances, even if your listing excluded them. All of these things you will have to weigh carefully against your need to get out.

- In a down market, the price may not be what you want, but try to ensure you get a substantial down payment and a stipulation that in the case the buyer does not complete the deal (it happens often in a falling market), the money is not returned but instead becomes your property.

- One strategy you might be forced into (although I would avoid it, if possible) is to offer financing in order to sell. This would usually be in the form of a VTB (vendor take-back) mortgage, which means instead of giving you the purchase price in cash on closing, the buyer hands over a smaller amount and you provide a mortgage for the rest. Normally a vendor will do this only when interest rates are high, and climbing, and the buyer wants to cut financing costs. But these days, the opposite is true as rates crash and central bankers try to encourage borrowing and invest-ing. So, chances are your purchaser just doesn't qualify for bank financing—and I doubt you will ever see all the cash.

- If there is a home inspection involved, hang around while it's taking place. In case deficiencies are found, it's good for you to know that for obvious reasons. You can also ask the home inspector direct questions about the problems, the remedies, and the approximate cost. That way you and your agent can bargain more effectively if the offer comes back for a reduced amount, reflecting the cost of repairs to the purchaser.

- Go for the shortest closing possible, even if it means you move out in a panic. For reasons already mentioned, I believe the housing market will decline for quite some time to come, so why give the buyer time to reconsider, get cold feet, and back out?

- If the deal does go south, know your options. You can sue the purchaser, but that takes months to wind its way through the process, and you might be stuck giving a litigation lawyer a $5,000 retainer before it even starts. So, far better to work with an offer to ensure both parties agree, that you get a sizeable amount of cash upfront, and get the thing shut down as soon as possible.

- Recognize that you might have to bribe a potential buyer to turn him or her into a real one. These days new home developers are giving away free finished basements or new cars, so odds are you might have to compete. Throwing in appliances is a start, and you might also have to spring for a year's worth of lawn maintenance or monthly condo fees. Cars are also a great incentive, but be aware with the kind of market we're walking into, buyers will still lowball you on prices.

- A final option is always an auction. They're not common in Canada yet, but that will change. Just make sure you have a reserve price. Booze might help, too.

After the crash, real estate's a financial loser

In case you missed my point by now: Real estate's a losing financial proposition. Consider it shelter, or get out. The market will not be advancing for several years, which means the cost of home ownership is a burden not worth bearing for most families. You are far better advised to:

- Live frugally and intelligently
- Save as much money as possible
- Invest in financial assets once the economic storm has passed
- View real estate as shelter

Residential real estate will decline for at least two full years following the crash of 2008, and then flatline for several more, perhaps through 2015. There's no serious money to be made on this asset, and lots to be lost. I seriously question the financial validity of owning a property as opposed to renting the same home.

For example, consider a homeowner with a $300,000 mortgage at 7 percent, with a long amortization and a property worth $400,000 when purchased. Financing payments equal more than $23,000 a year, 87 percent of which is interest. Five years later, the property owner has made $115,000 in debt service payments, of which over $100,000 was interest. During that time, the mortgage principal has been reduced to just over $280,000. If the owner is able to sell for what was paid for the house, it means he spent $100,000 over sixty months to rent $280,000. And this does not take into consideration insurance, maintenance, or property taxes. None of those costs would have been incurred to rent the same place.

Which begs the question: Why on earth would you do that? In the absence of any potential capital gain, it's a losing proposition.

This is why, after the crash, renters rule.

Face it: home ownership is no holy grail, no measure of accomplishment, and no accurate gauge of who you are. It's as meaningful and deep as fashion. At the end of the day, it's shelter. It should please you as well as protect you, but it should never become a wealth trap. Like every other asset, it rises and falls in value. Unlike most assets, however, it's too easily imbued with human emotion, and that messes everything up. We're entering a long period in which this misaffection will be painfully obvious and during which tenants will be the beneficiaries.

This is so basic it shouldn't even be a rule:
Buy assets which rise in value. Rent ones which fall.

This is why you lease your car, after all, and your office photo-copier. It should be the way you own computers, BlackBerries, your water heater, and other stuff which you know will be worth less (if anything) in five years.

In a deflationary world, renting is one of the sanest things you can possibly do, especially when owning something also means taking on a debt obligation. And especially a debt which is amortized over 20 or 30 years, the payments on which are 90 percent interest. That is a financial death wish.

Need more convincing?

Well, we are now entering the golden age of the renter. Market rents, already softening, will be plunging in most urban centres as the number of empty houses and condos explodes. This is a certainty for a couple of good reasons:

- We're at the bitter end of a real estate boom which—as all housing booms do—spawned an orgy of over-building. Developers scrambled madly to throw up new towers and pave over acres of fine farmland with driveways for minivans. Part-time, novice, greedy, or simply dumb speculators poured in after them, snapping up these units, often when they only existed on a website.

  Toronto gives us a good example of this, where more than 50,000 condo units were in the pipeline when the music died in mid-2008. Some of those were pre-sales in buildings which will never be lifted off the drawing board, some in developments which are big holes in the downtown landscape, destined now to be parking lots, some in towers too far along to be abandoned, and tens of thousands more built and occupied. In 2007, for example, a stunning 22,654 condos were sold and delivered in Toronto—a number that dwarfed development in Chicago or New York, according to research company Urbanation. Hard numbers are not easy to find, but it appears between 30 percent and 40 percent of all those units designed, created, built, or sold in the years after 2004 were bought by flippers. These folks never intended on moving in or even closing the deal, if they didn't have to. Instead, they banked on quick price appreciation in a condo-crazed, rising market and then a sale with a capital gain.

And the same happened in Calgary and Vancouver, where the second half of 2008 was marked by the cancellation of some very high-profile condo tower developments both downtown and in the 'burbs. And this is one reason rents in those three cities, and elsewhere, will be consistently falling—tens of thousands of empty condos owned by reluctant landlords. They were forced to close the deals, forced to pay closing costs, forced now into mortgage payments, condo or strata fees, and property tax bills. They're not at all happy about it, desperately seeking tenants, and happy to get any income to cut their monthly operating losses.

Already you can see the impact this is having, as renters in Toronto are offered months of free rent, free parking, free health club memberships and free decorating. Not only that, but rents are falling now, in some markets on a weekly basis. If your goal is to live the beautiful life in a swank urban building, save your money and be heavily subsidized by some hapless schmuck whose greed bit him, well, enjoy.

• The same holds true to an extent in the single-family home market, where many distressed homeowners now realize it was a mistake to buy. This is a direct consequence of banks, lenders, and regulators having let the bar for homeownership dip so low that getting a house became a right instead of a privilege. This is the legacy of zero-down payments and 40-year mortgages, which encouraged people without money to become owners.

Now that the market's turned, values are dropping and For Sale signs are cropping up along windy suburban streets like mushrooms after a torrent; reality has set in. Buying a house without money becomes a major monthly financial burden, once those novice homeowners understand the impact of

debt financing, property tax, insurance, utilities, and maintenance. So, they sell. But in this market, where sales are
increasingly hard to come by, they also rent. As with the condo
flippers, any relief from monthly obligations is welcome.

For example, in the western suburbs of Toronto there are
hundreds of homes for lease—virtually new houses which in
mid-2008 were worth $450,000 or $500,000, but can be rented
as I write this for $1,600 to $1,800 a month. To buy the same
house, even at a deep discount, would take a minimum of
$30,000 down (5 percent payment plus closing costs) and
monthly costs of $2,700. In addition, there is risk—tons of it.
In a deflating economy, the house could be worth $300,000 or
less in two years, and still have $380,000 in financing on it, for
which the owner is 100 percent responsible (and has paid
$40,000 in interest). Remember, there are no short sales here,
as in the US.

So, you can see how things have turned dramatically in favour of
tenants. In fact, renting will soon be a mark of financial acumen,
as the realization sets in that reluctant landlords are actually sub-
sidizing tenants to the tune of thousands of dollars a year.
Besides, if the goal in life is to live beyond your means and
become more financially secure while you do so, why wouldn't
you do this?

In addition, the law is shamelessly on the side of renters in
most jurisdictions. In Ontario and Quebec for example, it's
almost impossible for a landlord to get a tenant out of a condo or
a house once they occupy it. Even if a lease expires, it's considered to roll immediately into a monthly contract, extending to
the renter every right he or she had under the longer arrange-
ment, including extremely limited rent increases (except in the
case of first-occupied units, like new condos). In order to dis-
lodge a tenant, an owner has to prove he or she is going to gut

and renovate the unit or move in personally (or a family member). Establishing that can take a trip to court—a costly move most small landlords don't take.

This last point is just to counter the drippy, emotive nonsense argument I hear all the time in favour of buying and against renting—that an owner can sell a unit or just change his mind about renting it, and force a family onto the street. Anyone who believes that has read too many Dickens novels.

If you believe, as I do, that our greatest enemy is deflation and its firmest hold will be on real estate, then you are further ahead financially to rent shelter than own it. This will increase your monthly cash flow, allow you to establish a savings program, and position you much better to buy into the housing market (if you feel brave) in four or five years when the storm has passed and a new era of government-induced inflation is upon us.

And as market rents fall over the next couple of years, they will also be indicating the general decline in real estate values. One way of gauging that is with the Price/Rent Ratio.

THE P/R RATIO

The Price-to-Rent ratio has been used for some time to figure out if a piece of real estate is fairly valued relative to its ability to earn income in the marketplace. It operates on the same principle as a stock's P/E ratio. With stocks, investors can judge if the price being asked is worth paying based on what a single share yields. If the price is expensive and the earnings low, then the P/E is high—not a good thing for short-term capital gains. With a house, same thing. If the asking price or current market valuation bears an unrealistic relationship to what it can be rented for, it's probably not worth what the vendor is asking.

Here's how to determine that: simply take the annual rental income and divide it into the property's price tag, and then measure it against an historic norm. One good benchmark, according to Moody's Economy.com, is a P/R of 16—which is a long-term average. So, let's take one of the subdivision homes (of the kind mentioned above) in a western suburb of Toronto built three years ago, sitting on a 36-foot-wide lot with a double car garage, and on the market for $460,000. You can rent that three-bedroom home (or a mess of others just like it) for no more than $1,800 a month.

So, that's a yearly rental income of $21,600, divided into an asking price of $460,000, for a P/R ratio of 21.2. Ouch! This baby is overpriced, especially so because comparable houses can be leased for up to $300 a month less in the same general area. So, let's ask that other question: Is it better financially (i.e. cheaper) to buy or to rent this particular house?

Here's the simple math on 20 percent down (that's $92,000) and a mortgage of $368,000, plus maintenance costs, insurance and property taxes (charges not incurred by a tenant).

- Down payment cost (what $92,000 a year would earn in a 3 percent GIC): $2,760
- Mortgage payments ($368,000 at 5-yr rate of 7.2 percent, 25-year amortization): $31,477
- Maintenance (new house, virtually nothing): $1,000
- Insurance: $1,700
- Property tax (in this area, average on 3-bedroom, 2,000-sq-ft home): $5,400
- Total annual ownership cost: $42,377
- Rental cost for the same house: $21,600
- Annual cost of being a Greater Fool: ($20,737)

Finally, on renting versus owning, here's a comment I agree with, made by Yale economist Robert Shiller, one of the smartest guys around these days: "As any classical economist will tell you, homeownership is actually not a great idea from an investment standpoint. A better strategy would be to diversify as much as possible—put your money into stocks, bonds, many different geographies—then use the income to rent whatever you like, which allows for greater flexibility and efficiencies. The popular argument that renting is equivalent to throwing money down the drain is really fallacious, since the money you save can be used to produce dividends."

IN PRAISE OF VULTURES

A few words now on being a contrarian (which I greatly admire), and on actually buying real estate in this deflationary environment. Is this a completely wingy idea?

Well, the headlines, economic indicators and prevailing investor sentiment would scream "yes, you're an idiot!" but there's always a strong case to be made for buying assets when they're most unloved. Today real estate—residential and commercial—is definitely in that category, for all the reasons I have indicated above. Anybody thinking of taking the plunge must do so in the expectation that a property could well be worth less in a year than it is on the day of closing. That means you have to buy as cheaply as possible, with the terms solidly in your favour to mitigate against additional market declines. It's called being a vulture. Some might use the term "bottom-feeder," but I prefer a more lofty view.

In the US, especially in those areas most decimated by the real estate implosion—California, Arizona, Florida—vulture investment funds have sprung up which are amassing housing units and development land at what they think are generationally low prices. Some of these are commercial ventures, while others operate as investment clubs. All of them are brave, since it seems the housing floor will not be touched until late 2009 at the earliest or more likely sometime in 2010. But, of course, there will be a rebound, even if it takes until 2015 or later to get back to 2006 price levels (if that ever happens).

The real estate market will never die, of course. But it will change. Some of the themes I have written about here—the inevitable demise of the suburbs and the rise of energy consciousness, for example—will greatly impact the market value of housing going forward. Some kinds of homes, like the Baby Boomer five-bedroom excessive specials, are simply destined for

abandonment or tear-downs. But by the same token, as the deflationary pendulum swings, some properties will fall in value so
disastrously they become irresistible as speculative investments
to those contrarians among us.

How to be a Vulture

Here are some tips for would-be vultures. Enjoy the carrion.

- Offer what you want to pay, not what the vendor is asking
  to be paid. With so many properties listed, and so little
  sales activity, every offer has to be taken seriously. Only by
  writing up an offer on your own terms, at your own prices,
  will you get a sign-back showing the true level of despera-
  tion you're dealing with.
- Always submit the offer with a deposit cheque, which is like
  putting a shiny lure on the end of your fishing line.
  However, the offer must stipulate the cheque is not cashable
  until a firm and binding agreement is reached. So, it means
  nothing, while having a powerful psychological impact.
- Throw in as many conditions as you want. This will create
  an offer that is completely tailored to your needs and wants
  while providing elements you can remove in order to gain
  things you truly want. So, for example, make the offer conditional on the vendors paying all your closing costs,
  including land transfer tax. While you never expect that to
  happen, you can remove it during negotiations in order to
  get what you do want and expect, which is a bargain price.
- Ditto for conditions giving you time to arrange financing or
  even to sell another property—they are both traditional
  deal-breakers, and the vendor's agent will know that immediately. So, by reluctantly removing them you move far
  closer to getting that price.
- Best, however, to insist on a home inspection. This condition should give you five business days to complete the
  process, and is normally done at the purchaser's expense.

The reason you want this is because almost all properties need some kind of work done in order to make them perfect, and when you get the inspector's report you have leverage to help you drive down the price. Simply get an estimate of the cost of the repairs and ask for the deal to be rewritten with a price reduced by that amount. Since the vendor knows the condition is entirely for your benefit and the deal will die unless you sign a waiver, well, guess what? Vulture.

- And remember that the closing date is also an important poker chip to play. Have your agent find out what the vendor wants, and then use that to help leverage the price down. Additionally, you can throw any assets you see around the property into your offer—power tools, appliances, lawn tractor, Harley-Davidson, whatever. The most you put in, the more clutter there is for the vendor to wade through, and the better chance you have of securing the best deal.

- Speaking of which, why not make two offers at the same time on two competing properties, and then let that fact be known (through your agent) to the vendor? That will add even more pressure to the poor guy, as he tries to figure out what he must do to save the deal, and give you what you want. This may be cruel and unusual, but just consider it payback for all those multiple-offer situations greedy vendors placed buyers in during the bubble years.

- And, of course, you can make a lowball offer, get a signback, and then just let it die. Wait a week and go back in with another one, for the same low price. Odds are you will not get the same response this time. The stressed-out vendor may hate you, but he'll close.

AND WHAT'S WORTH BUYING? REAL ESTATE WITH A FUTURE.

Here are some guidelines:

1. Avoid the suburbs, especially those developed within the past five years. There are many reasons, several of which have already been touched upon—like remoteness, lack of shopping and other services, lack of human scaling, a dependence on cars, cheap building materials, no trees (adds to energy costs in summer), lots too small for gardens and zoning restrictions against outside storage or generators and excessive floor plans, not to mention out-of-control property taxes in most suburban municipalities trying to pay for insane growth since 2000.
2. Avoid ghettos of newly-built houses. In addition to the points above, these suckers will have marginal resale value even after real estate values stabilize and economic confidence is restored. They lack architectural interest, are squashed together on marginal lots miles away from places of employment, are situated on streets devoid of focus and are convenient to nothing. These are the problem-plagued neighbourhoods of the future, where social breakdown is first likely to occur. Stay clear.
3. Buy small. Given what's coming in our immediate future, and what the years following 2015 will bring, the most in-demand real estate will be smart houses of manageable size. Nobody will care more about having granite, glass, or marble counter-tops than geothermal heating, a greywater recycling system or, especially, an appropriate and cost-effective amount of space. Bungalows, townhomes, and duplexes (providing predictable income) in established urban neighbourhoods or smaller cities and towns will command a premium. Condos will be valued based on the carrying costs, security, location, and population mix of owners. In general, the amount of space people choose to live in will shrink—back to the 1,000 square feet that was once considered absolutely adequate for a family of three. (Family size will fall, too,)

4. Buy energy efficiency. Although the deflationary times cover over the environmental crisis with an economic and financial one, this will change in the years to come. Peak oil, new tariffs and taxes on energy consumption, a massive jump in natural gas costs, disruptions in the delivery of electricity, heavy user fees on the provision of clean water and the treatment of sewage, transportation and gas levies—all of this will change home-buying tastes dramatically. Boomers who delay unloading their big, leaky, suburban houses, for example, will find virtually no buyers—and if they do, receive just pennies on each dollar of equity they invested. Remember, all home energy costs—electricity, gas, heating oil—could double or triple in cost within ten years. Just remember what $1.40-a-litre gasoline did to SUV sales and the big car companies, and assume the same will be happening to those big homes we all lusted after a few short years ago.

5. Buy climate smart. No leaky condos in BC (no, not the old leaky ones—the new leaky ones). No farmland in Saskatchewan. No coastal retreats in Nova Scotia or PEI. If you want water, find an inland lake.

6. Buy simplicity. No in-ground pools, requiring pumps, filters, buckets of chemicals, and little buildings to put them in. No acres of grass to cut. No hot tubs, media rooms, or excessive plumbing. Buy a place with room for a clothesline, and room for canine security.

7. Buy self-sufficiency. A big premium will be happily paid by future buyers for a home that can double as a fortress against a return to deflationary times or the arrival of the new environmental realities. Thus, pay attention to heat, power, water, and food. That means a woodstove (or pellets), solar-assisted heat source, geothermal system, a generator (gasoline, propane or natural gas), well and land for growing vegetables, having fruit trees, or converting feed into protein (aka chickens). Even if such measures are not required for day-to-day life, the fact that a property offers them will increase its worth in the marketplace to come.

8. Buy as many of these features as possible: Insulated concrete foundations, solar panels or coils, rainwater collection/irrigation system, high-efficiency windows, doors, multi-fuel furnace, permeable surface driveway, organic paints and adhesives, a community.

9. Concentrate on properties people will want as primary residences. Forget about cottages, chalets, and other recreational lands. These are generally the first to be decimated in value in an economic downturn and the last to recover. Incredibly, 40 percent of all equity borrowing in the US in the few years before the crash was to purchase second properties, which is one reason the market there has been destroyed. In Canada, most cottages are financed with equity loans taken against city properties, so as the deflationary storm hits, owners will be trying to bail out of those obligations at any cost. But, don't bite—not unless you are prepared to sit on your investment for years, maybe a decade.

10. Tempted by all those massive price reductions in Florida or California? Do your vulture hormones vibrate at the thought of picking up a foreclosure high atop a cliff in Malibu? Take a cold shower. Realize there's got to be a powerful reason smart people who live in the San Francisco or Miami areas are not snapping up distressed properties with gay abandon, and why US realtors and brokers spend so much time and money targeting Canadians as potential marks for unloved houses in their communities.

When it comes to property—especially what might seem tempting bargains—the truth is, a lot of property out there has no future. US housing prices are nowhere near the bottom, and won't get there until 2010, or beyond—depending on the depths of the economic valley that country is travelling into. Why would you buy a piece of property for 15 percent more than it might be worth in a year? That the locals won't touch with a barge pole? What makes you so smart? Besides, have you done your homework? If you buy and rent out a home in the States, you must report the rental income on both sides of the border, and the sale of an US property means you are subject to a withholding tax on the proceeds large enough to nuke most profits (should you be so lucky).

In addition, there's a lot of other trouble this strategy can get you into, as a *US News* report spelled out. For example, each American state has its own laws governing foreclosures, which means a contract to purchase one requires very specific expertise to keep it from going afoul of the law. As the president of Foreclosures.com pointed out, "If you don't have the language proper in your contract, or if you have even the font size wrong, it's criminal, and civil damages—don't count on every realtor knowing this." That means paying not only a real estate guy for local knowledge, but also hiring a local lawyer to guide the transaction.

Buying a foreclosure also means making darn sure you can hold on for a decade, at least. Forget thinking about any quick flip, unless you like losing lots of money. Then there's the condition of most foreclosed properties, which is generally appalling. And why not? Would you keep the furnace in good repair, re-shingle the roof or battle insect pests in a home you knew you'd be defaulting on in a few months? The general rule of thumb is to have 10 percent of the purchase price available for emergency repairs, unless you like termites a lot.

11. If you do decide to invest in real estate anywhere during these precarious times, and plan to use borrowed money, be careful. Get pre-approved for financing, so you have a good idea of how much financing you're good for. Second, always opt for a variable-rate mortgage, instead of one with a rate and payment amounts fixed for a long period of time, typically five years. While we all like stability, the fact is interest rates will be held at absurdly low levels for the next few years, and decline close to the zero mark as central bankers and bankrupt governments try everything possible to kick-start economic growth. By having a variable-rate loan, you will benefit from

the trip down and if rates start to increase again, you can always lock in with a phone call.

Here's a bit of my previous mortgage advice, which is more relevant now than ever, because debt is a killer during deflationary times, and you need to use every tool possible to kill it off. Use every trick you can to speed the repayment process, since this saves bundles of precious money. One is to make pre-payments, lump sum payments, whenever your lender allows it—typically up to 10 per cent or 15 per cent of the loan once a year. Another is to increase monthly payments over the required amount, with the surplus coming right off the principal outstanding.

The best method of killing off a mortgage I know, is too dump your monthly payments and replace them with weekly ones. By accelerating payments to this frequency, you will pay off the loan in a shockingly short period of time and save tens of thousands, maybe hundreds of thousands, in interest. Take the usual monthly payment, divide it by four, and arrange with your bank to have that taken from you account every seven days. By doing so, you'll be making the equivalent of one extra monthly payment a year, with excellent results. By quickening the reduction of the principal, you slow the accumulation of new interest and see a dramatic increase in equity.

I've spent a little more time in this book on residential real estate than any other asset classes for a simple and profound reason: We have too much of it. It now imperils us, and has been the leading agent of deflation in the US. This was only starting to be the case in the early months of 2009, and will be a defining factor affecting most Canadians in the years ahead. We, too, have irresponsibly inflated home values. Our government, equally, was to blame for bad policies and slipshod regulation. Our bankers jumped into securitization and the sale of lousy mortgages right along with the colleagues on Wall Street and in The

City. All the toxic chickens have come flocking home.

Now, as we face global deflation led by the faltering Chinese economy and unemployment levels which could rival those of the 1930s, millions of Canadian families need to get their finances in order. With more than 80 percent of household net worth still sitting in real estate, this is the first place to start. For some, selling as quickly as possible is the best option, escaping debt and becoming renters. For others, using every tool and strategy possible to pay down debt will help them weather the storm. Scores of Baby Boomers need to act fast. Lots of folks with expensive houses waiting for the market to improve before selling need to know that it won't.

While we all need houses to live in, and while real estate will always be wanted, our collective greed and lust have poisoned this asset for a long time to come. When you look at Robert Shiller's chart of US house prices over the last 130 years you can see easily how we created one of the largest financial bubbles of all time, adding trillions of dollars of worth to residential properties. The sad part is that most of the new wealth did not come from increased prosperity—wages and profits—but rather from debt. When any bubble bursts, money fades.

But the financing remains.

This overhang of debt comes at the worst of times. The global financial system is more fragile and weak than Canadians imagined. The American economy is in tatters, its industry faltering and its future now more indebted than ever. The ripples have impacted most countries, which hurts trade and threatens to create a global downturn which so easily can devolve into a depression. The crash of 2008 was not the conclusion of a bad time, but the beginning of one. Now we have falling assets, weaker banks, hobbled markets, negative growth, and rising unemployment to deal with. These are the conditions which turn the wrong real estate from an asset into a serious liability. And on the horizon are the other three crises we need to prepare for— the age wave, peak oil, and climate change.

As dismal as this sounds, it's far from hopeless. People survived times just as challenging in the past by taking action, not just taking cover.

No matter what the next few years bring (and it won't be pretty or predictable), you must seize control.

CHAPTER FIVE

CAUTIOUS AND AUDACIOUS: THE REALITY OF THE NEW ECONOMY

When I drive through the suburbs outside Toronto, Halifax, or Calgary, the satellite cities around Vancouver, or the acres of instant homes now crowding Kitchener or Winnipeg, there's often a troubling image in my mind of want amid prosperity. In all directions, there are new homes and new cars, new fast food restaurants, new big box retailers, new schools, new saplings, and new asphalt. But behind everything to be seen is a well of debt, credit, and obligation.

The people who live here, average middle-class families, are among the billion on earth who are part of the First World. Two billion more, principally in China and India, are working their way into this category, and three billion others just try to survive. But how insulated are we, the privileged few, from the daily struggle most of the world's population faces?

The crash of 2008 says the gap is far narrower that appearances suggest. Suddenly you realize there's a chance your mortgage might not be automatically renewed by a bank that needs the cash; that the big company you bought your car from mightn't be around to repair it; that one day at Loblaws your credit card could be declined, permanently; that your home, when you come to sell, could be worth less than what you owe on it; that a stock market decline lasting a year could erase your RRSP; or that, through no fault of your own, you could lose your job.

Each of these possibilities is no longer remote. In fact, one or two will happen to most Canadian families. And most families won't be ready. This leads to my image of streets full of nice houses with new cars surrounded with many stores, and yet citizens in despair and want amid apparent wealth. A similar thing was seen in the 1930s, despite the iconic vision we have of the tattered unemployed riding the top of boxcars. For most people going through the Depression, life was just a series of shocks and hardships. The shops were still full, people without jobs were still smart and sophisticated and the government still functioned. But average families saw their incomes drastically cut, the value of their assets wildly deflated, their houses losing most of their value, and employment prospects vanish. Deflation caused the value of cash to rise dramatically and men like my father were immensely happy to find work building what would be Highway 401, for $1 a day.

Because few people saw the Depression coming, few prepared. Had warning been given, they might have reduced spending, increased saving, sold their real estate, and done everything possible to build a reserve of liquid wealth. Few then, as now, could do much about corporate failures and massive unemployment. But even a few months to prepare could have made a huge difference to the quality of life when the times grew dark.

Today there are many insightful people who believe we are at a similar point. But there is one great difference making our current situation more dangerous, which is debt.

Never before have families owed so much on their credit cards, car loans, mortgages, student loans, lines of credit, and personal borrowings as today. Everyone must adopt strategies to deal with this, immediately.

In the 1930s, after all, there was no plastic, no home equity lines of credit, no 95 percent mortgage financing, and no do-not-pay-until-2012 plasma TV and leather living room suite deals. Nobody I can find bought their homes in the 1920s with nothing down, got 0 percent financing on a vehicle, or graduated from university with $32,000 in loans. Quite apart from the debt quagmire governments and corporations are currently in, average Canadian families are on balance much more at risk than they were on October 28, 1929, or prior to the second wave of collapse in the late spring of 1930.

This book is aimed at correcting that, as much as possible, for those people paying attention. Hopefully we'll not see recession become a deflationary spiral down. But there's an even more remote chance things will stay the same. Common sense and the instinct for survival dictate you have to make at least some changes—and as quickly as possible—to prepare for an altered world. In the next chapter I provide checklists of actions to take, depending on your own weighting of the risks I have presented. In the meantime, there are two final areas you must reflect on and assess:

WHERE IS MONEY SAFE?

Your choices are stark. Most often money resides in the form of:

- Invested wealth—stocks, bonds, mutual funds or various market alternatives
- Near cash, like savings accounts or guaranteed investment certificates
- Cash in your pocket, safety deposit box, or home safe
- Real estate or corporate equity
- Physical assets like cars, boats, airplanes, or art
- Precious metals

We will deal with wealth invested in market securities in a few pages. Cash held in its physical form and readily accessible (at hand) is clearly the primary repository of wealth for most people, but it is not safe from theft or loss unless you take the measures described earlier. But this much is clear: Everyone should have a cash reserve in days like these. As for physical money given to a bank for safekeeping, safety deposit boxes are largely immune from even a bank failure, but not from bank theft (a very unlikely occurrence).

Money on deposit involves trust in both the bank and the federal agency which guarantees that sum, the CDIC (Canada Deposit Insurance Corporation). Deposit insurance was one of the reforms which came out of the Great Depression, when a run on the banks by worried savers led to bank failures, forced closures, and financial ruin. The last thing our banks could withstand now, in their highly leveraged state, would be for a few million people to ask for their money back. To prevent that from (ever) happening, governments have offered to guarantee—to a limit—all your savings. The idea is to prevent you from actually getting that money into your possession, and out of circulation.

In the immediate aftermath of the crash of 2008, a global run on the banks was a distinct and growing possibility, especially as news reports spread of worried people in Iceland, Britain, and other countries storming their financial institutions. That prompted a number of governments to rush in with new guarantees. The European Union, for example, raised the guarantee offered deposits from a low of US $27,000 to a standard $68,000. Australia said it would guarantee any sized deposit, but sums over $1 million would be charged an insurance fee. The US jumped its guarantee to $250,000 for individual deposits, with separate insurance covering retirement and investment accounts. Canada refused to raise the CDIC limits.

Here's the protection Canadians receive:
- A maximum of $100,000 per person, per bank
- This is the total of any and all savings or chequing

accounts, term deposits, or GICs of five years or less.
- Open a joint account with your spouse, and get another $100,000.
- Your spouse or child can be covered for an equal and separate amount.
- No deposits in foreign currencies are guaranteed.
- No stocks, bonds, treasury bills, or mutual fund amounts are eligible.
- RRSPs or RRIFs to $100,000 are covered, but only if invested in eligible assets, like savings deposits or GICs.

An obvious strategy then, for those fortunate enough to have hundreds of thousands in cash: Spread it around and open joint accounts. But, should this reassure? Not according to Eric Sprott, head of Toronto-based Sprott Asset Management. Here's what he told his clients while those anxious governments were sweet-talking the world's savers:

> Like it or not, in the financial world everything is someone else's liability and every financial asset has default risk. Even cash under the mattress is someone else's liability . . . it's the liability of the central bank. Which is why nobody should be breathing a sigh of relief that central banks are now guaranteeing everything. They guaranteed all bank deposits. They guaranteed money market funds. They guaranteed inter-bank lending. But at what cost?
>
> As they are wont to do, they only traded one problem for another. For what does a government guarantee really mean? It means they are the buyer of last resort for other people's liabilities. It means they are ready, willing, and able to print money in any quantity to back the guarantee. It means they are trying to solve the problem of default risk by causing the equally nefarious problem of purchasing power/inflation risk. (Conversely they could tax their

citizenry into oblivion, but this would be much less politically acceptable than printing money, especially in a debtor nation such as the US.) During times of financial crisis, it is best not to trust anybody, especially not the central banks.

Immediately following the crash, governments indeed went on an orgy of guarantees, bailouts, and rescues. Washington alone was on the hook for $7 trillion by the final days of 2008, and still the auto industry teetered on the brink of collapse, while millions of Americans were on track to lose their homes and default on their residential mortgages. Just imagine if President Obama disappoints in his first term, the financial situation worsens, more banks fail, markets take a Depression-style additional crash, and the real estate market is hit with that second wave of deflation just as the unemployment rate is charging into double-digits. Will folks trust the government to safeguard their remaining wealth? More importantly, if there were a run on the banks, could Washington backstop it?

Of course not. Barack Obama would do just what FDR did, and temporarily shut the banks to save them.

And in Canada, there is a similar dilemma. While citizens here are constantly told our banking system is far more stable than that of many other countries, this does not mean it is inherently safer. In fact, rumours on Bay Street persist that at least one of our Big Five banks has already raised the alarm in Ottawa. In fact, the finance minister in late 2008 admitted that, "We've had a couple of financial institutions in Canada that ran the risk of falling outside the capitalization requirements. We required them ... to maintain the appropriate capital requirements and raise capital as necessary, which was done months ago."

While the specific banks were not mentioned, one was likely CIBC, which was badly burned in the US subprime mortgage mess, leading to losses of more than $3 billion in 2008, after profits of $2.4 billion the year before. The bank was forced to raise

$2.75 billion in new capital in 2008 by selling off stock at a sharp discount, and raised concerns that senior executives had taken extreme risks.

And, don't forget, Ottawa engineered its own bailout of the Canadian banks in 2008 with a stunning $75 billion purchase of residential mortgages through its agency, the Canada Mortgage and Housing Corporation. This effectively took those mortgages—which CMHC had already guaranteed (since they were high-ratio borrowings by homeowners with little equity)—off the banks' books and replaced them with cash, a move the government said was necessary because, "we will not allow Canada's financial system, which has been ranked as the soundest in the world, to be put at risk by global events."

"At a time of considerable uncertainty in global financial markets, this action will provide Canada's financial institutions with significant and stable access to longer-term funding," the finance minister of the day told reporters.

But if Canada has such a sound banking system, why a bailout that in terms of our population and economy, is actually larger than the massive $700 billion the US Congress set aside to stabilize its banking system? And while American politicians wrestled over that rescue package, almost failing to pass it amid a widespread popular protest, why was a similar move in this country not debated or even submitted to Parliament? Should that lack of scrutiny and transparency raise concerns among depositors that the Canadian banking system is a lot more porous and wobbly than the central government is letting on?

What if there was a run on the CIBC, for example? There are chequing accounts worth $32 billion and savings accounts worth $44 billion in this one bank alone, money which could be withdrawn almost instantly. Even if a small amount of that $76 billion was taken out in a week, the bank would be insolvent, seeing it has less than $1.5 billion in cash. Would Ottawa just write a cheque for the other $75 billion to ensure the Bank of Commerce was kept standing? Even though it is out of money, now running a budget deficit, and such an amount of money would equal 40 percent of its annual budget? Is this believable?

Meanwhile, what's backing those Canadian dollars? The power to tax. That's it. This is called "fiat currency" because it has been created by a government order (or fiat), and is not convertible into anything else. This is the reality today for global currencies, including the US dollar, which all have fluctuating values relative to each other, as currency traders worry about factors like relative economic strength.

Because our bank notes are not convertible, rapid changes in their value are possible and can wreak havoc. In 2008, for example, the Canadian dollar bounced between $1.10 US and 80 cents as the financial crisis rolled in. That made it virtually impossible for importers and exporters to plan their revenues and expenditures and massively changed many consumer prices. Scarier is what happens to the currencies of economies in trouble, as poor Icelanders found out when a banking crisis hit and the krona lost 80 percent of its value. Many people there had taken loans and mortgages in euros to reduce interest charges, and ended up being nailed as a result. Also, in the final months of that year, national currencies in Brazil and Mexico were pounded, along with that of South Korea and several European nations.

These are the factors, then, that after the crash have led a growing number of people to turn their back on government-backed cash and bank deposits:

Not so safe as cash in the bank?

- Government deposit guarantees would wither in the heat of a bank run
- Banks would become rapidly insolvent in a crisis of confidence
- Bailouts by Washington and Ottawa raise doubts over bank stability
- Rapid and uncontrollable currency fluctuations are increasingly common

- Nothing stands behind our paper money
- What option would you have in the event of a forced "bank holiday"?

These are some of the reasons why precious metals, gold in particular, are considered by lots of people—now more than ever—to be the most secure assets on earth for the preservation of wealth. Gold has been a traditional storehouse of value and an alternative currency for thousands of years, even though the metal has little practical or industrial use (other than in your jewellery and computer). Despite that, it has been coveted through the centuries and has the two advantages of being universally accepted, and highly portable. Many generations of people under stress have been able to survive, or at least improve their lot, by having tradable gold in their possession.

Could that be in our future? Some hunks of gold for a tank of gasoline? A side of beef? How much for a house?

Because gold has also been an alternative to paper money (except in those times when cash was convertible into gold, and governments used the "gold standard" to back the paper they issued) it has historically risen in value when cash declines in worth. Thus, when inflation erodes a dollar, an ounce of gold grows more dear. But what of today? No inflation. Instead we have seriously deflating assets—houses, corporations, commodities including oil—so why should gold not also be falling?

Simply because we're in uncharted territory. A global debt and credit crisis of historic proportions has led to a loss of confidence in the entire banking and financial sector, and fiat currency itself. As governments try to solve the problem, gambling more billions and trillions on rescue and stimulus packages, they increase the odds of a calamitous outcome. Since it is only government order that backs our currencies, what happens to the value of money if governments fail? Do you want to be left sitting on your net worth—if you're successful in getting it out of your real estate and the stock market—in paper money that suddenly won't buy much? After all, this is what helped turn the capital of Iceland— once full of bustling bars and restaurants—into an urban tomb.

In a credit crisis like this one, trust is a rare commodity, especially trust in politicians. Back to Eric Sprott, an avowed gold bug, who puts it this way:

> Today's financial system, with the institution of the central bank at its foundation, has proven to be anything but as stable and prosperous as once thought. For the first time in a long while, the very foundations of capitalism are being put into question. Once infallible central banks of developed nations have become almost irrelevant. The financial markets, even the stock markets, are completely ignoring them.
>
> Central banks have shown, to their chagrin, that they can only solve one problem by causing another. The system is in such a state of disarray that the leaders of many of the world's developed countries, including the US, Britain, France and others, are now proposing some sort of massive overhaul in the way the world does finance. How it will all play out remains to be seen. Certainly it will involve greater government involvement and therefore greater waste and inefficiency. But be that as it may, we would not consider any paper based asset as 'safe' right now. Especially not currencies . . . When the markets realize this, the outcome should be highly bullish for gold.

This is a world in which the bankers have so screwed things up with their collateralized debt obligations, securitized subprime mortgages, and derivatives like credit-default swaps that trust and quality have been wrung out of the system. Lending between banks froze up, leading governments to spend obscene amounts of money trying to thaw it, because nobody trusted the quality of anybody else's assets. And with trillions in toxic mortgages and massive bets made against future payments floating around, why would they?

To those who think gold is a better place to put wealth, even bank savings and chequing accounts are suspect. After all, if CIBC, for example, took in more than $70 billion in such money and yet has only $1.5 billion in cash, it means the rest was loaned out. As what? Mortgages to young couples in Markham who bought big houses and don't have any money? To Boomers in Kelowna whose homes are losing $10,000 a month in equity? Is that why Ottawa moved to snap up $75 billion in mortgages from the banks?

And while defenders of the system argue that such worries are baseless, that our banks are severely regulated and solid as the Canadian Shield, those who believe in bullion shrug such assurances off. Gold, says Sprott, "is the only asset that has absolutely no default risk whatsoever and . . . is the only true safe haven asset." In the long run, the bullion believers say, countries like the US cannot possibly meet their financial obligations. Paying back the trillions being borrowed now will lead to more inflation and eroded dollars. Plus, there are massive obligations in store to cope with the age wave of retiring Baby Boomers, and the unfunded pension obligations that will wash into the government's hands as corporate giants fall in the wake of the crash. Gold, they say, is the only refuge. People will become fearful of paper money, and where else will there be to hide?

GOLD: REFUGE IN UNCERTAIN TIMES

Speaking of hiding money, a few words about Elgin, my brother, sadly dead.

He lived a storied and rebellious life. In high school my parents tried to mollify him with a new car. He got in, drove from Toronto to southern Florida, worked his way to Cuba on a banana boat, and became a fighter in Castro's 1958 revolution. He showed up months later at the front door with a machete in his belt and a monkey on his shoulder. (The little beast later jumped on a high-voltage electrical wire and was fried.)

That adventure set the tone for the rest of his life, some of it too graphic for a financial book (ask me about the hooker he brought home on Father's Day, when you see me next. She was so embarrassed she did the dishes.). Years later Elgin was operating out of Los Angeles, apparently making big money. So, he sent me a box full of it in Toronto, and asked me to go and buy a bar of gold, when bullion was all the rage and selling at that moment for about $700 US an ounce. So, I went to the city's premier gold dealer, walked past the security guards to the teller's cage and deposited my box.

One bar, please, I said. "Well that be a five-ounce bar, or ten?" she asked. No, I said, make it four hundred. And I shoved over the box full of US twenties. A few months later I received a phone call from Amsterdam, and my brother asked me to sell his bar. Gold was now at almost $850 an ounce, or $1,000 Canadian—and he had managed to hit the high-water mark. I went back to the teller's cage, and this time walked out with a money order in my pocket.

I am sure my brother enjoyed every penny of it prior to his premature death in Spain.

This small story illustrates simply how gold has been used over the centuries as a repository of wealth. This started about 3,000 BC, with gold jewellery in what is now Iraq, and was taken to an extreme in Ancient Egypt with King Tut's gold mask (which I will never forget seeing in person). Gold caused crazy Europeans to lurch across the Atlantic five hundred years ago in glorified fishing boats to plunder Incan and Aztec societies for their precious metals, and for almost 40 centuries gold coins and wafers formed the money supply in Europe, Britain, Asia, and then in young Canada.

From more than a decade before Confederation until the First World War, Canadian bank notes were backed by gold, which was kept for a while in big vaults in the basement of the East Block on Parliament Hill (I walked past them—now empty— every week as I took a shortcut through the tunnel under the front lawn over to Centre Block). Then, along with the US and much of the western world, Canada went off the gold standard in 1971. That's when Richard Nixon ended the practice of pegging the price of the metal (it was then at $42.22 US), and allowed private ownership of it. The world soon went bullion nuts. Today most governments, including Canada's, have sold off the bulk of their gold reserves, and the metal has seen increased industrial usage in electronics like computer boards, where it's prized for its conductive properties.

Canadians and Americans seem well aware of the worth and allure of gold, but own relatively little of it, putting far more faith in paper money and investment assets which these days are essentially collections of electrons. This differs from societies in India and China and the mid-East, for example, where gold equals real wealth, prized by families amassing wedding gifts or protecting assets from the vagaries of shifting currencies and suspect governments.

Today, of course, many people believe there are important new and sometimes contradictory reasons to possess bullion, and convert at least a portion of what you're worth into the gleaming, portable, yellow metal.

Why gold now seduces

- The destruction of financial markets by excessive debt and credit. Trillions in toxic assets and unresolved derivatives have yet to implode.
- A suspicion that the global banking system is far weaker than has been stated.
- The fear that massive government bailouts will eventually result in a new bout of inflation once this deflationary period is over, devaluing currencies, especially the US dollar.
- Major future tax increases to pay for bank rescues. Wealth in physical gold is not subject to income tax.
- The potential devaluation of more fiat currencies, including the loonie.

- The collapse of corporations, profits, and share values in a US-led depression, ushering in years more of a bear stock market.
- The loss of public confidence in paper money; a run on the banks
- The inevitability of serious energy inflation due to peak oil or a bigger mid-East war, disrupting crude supplies. Commodity price inflation will lift gold even higher.

Do you have a home safe? Does it contain enough cash to tide you and your family over for six months? Do you think it would be prudent to own gold as well, to protect a portion of your accumulated wealth against inflation, depression, or bank collapse?

Only you can answer such questions. If you have confidence in the status quo, don't bother with gold. If you fear the future, load up. If you simply believe we're in rapidly changing times and the future won't look like the past, then join lots of other people who, since the bottom fell out of the world as we knew it in September 2008, have become brand new gold owners.

Here is a glimpse into why that is happening, from one of the thousands of Internet chats among people who are convinced gold will be the only safe haven in the troubled years to come, and has already proved its worth countless times:

Unlike paper money, which can be printed up/entered into the computer on a whim, gold has a much more stable value. I say this because you cannot print up or enter into a computer account physical gold in that same manner. Expanding the gold supply is hard, dirty, dangerous work. People have gotten hurt, even died creating the money supply in mines, shipping channels, and refining plants. It takes time to make an ounce of gold or silver. On top of that, since nearly all the gold ever mined in the last 7,000 years remains aboveground, the annual addition to the gold supply only increases it by a small fraction, helping to keep the gold supply stable in terms of value, and that stable feature grows into the future as the gold supply grows larger.

You need to understand that the piece of paper that is a $100 bill cost only a few cents to make, no more than the $1 bill. That is what fiat means. Backed by nothing other than the faith of the US government and unconstitutional tender laws that say you can redeem a tattered dollar bill with another one. There is nothing in fiat currency to keep us honest, to keep the people close to the vest from taking advantage of inflation and working it to the common people's disadvantage. We cannot resist the temptation. It is part of human nature. History is littered with stories like this. The ancient Roman empire? Archaeologists in the last few years finally confirmed that the ancient government did indeed debase the currency by increasing the amount of base metals in what were originally gold and silver coins, and finally going to all-base-metal coins, even clipping the gold coins.

The Chinese experiment in paper money? They played with it for several centuries, having to reform it several times because of inflation.

The US Continental Dollar? "Not worth a continental" came out of the Revolutionary period. The Union green-backs? Used to fund the Civil War because gold couldn't be made fast enough to fund the war.

But even with all those compelling reasons to believe in gold, there are downsides to it as an investment:

- Gold is a speculative investment, not an income-producing one. It doesn't pay interest or dividends, only capital gains if you sell the metal for more than you paid.
- There are no tax benefits to owning gold, unlike, say, stocks, which produce dividend income. Gold is purchased with

after-tax dollars and there's nothing deductible about it.

- You cannot hold physical precious metals inside an RRSP—so, once again, the purchase cannot yield a tax advantage, like a stock or a mutual fund holding inside your retirement account. However, bullion certificates are permitted investments.

- You have to worry about purity since there are many different grades of gold on the market. This is why you should always (a) buy from a reputable, established, and large dealer (no, don't do it online), (b) get a certificate of purity from the refiner or assayer, or (c) opt for a gold coin issued by a sovereign government with a guaranteed gold content stamped on it.

- Once in your possession (unless you opt for a certificate of ownership), you have to worry about where to put it, and how to protect it. Thieves, robbers and bandits love bullion as much as you do, and for largely the same reasons. This means you must incur the cost of renting a safety deposit box, install an adequate safe in a secure location, or bury it in the backyard, preferably at night.

Despite these disadvantages, quietly, demand for physical gold in the final two months of 2008 was nothing short of spectacular, particularly for gold coins. This is not surprising, since in a time when gold might once again become an alternative currency, coins come with their own irrefutable authenticity. And this brings us to a few key questions: How much gold should you have? How should you own it? Where do you get it?

HOW MUCH GOLD SHOULD YOU OWN?

There are two answers to this. First, if you share the concerns listed above and think gold is a great insurance policy against dark days to come, a return of out-of-control inflation, or a simple caving-in of the world's financial system, then a consensus view is a minimum of 10 percent of your liquid net worth should be in gold. If you're really freaked out, double that. This is gold you hold permanently, never sell, and only add to. Stroke it every night if you find that reassuring—more than you can do with your life insurance policy.

Holding gold for profit is something else. This is obviously done if you believe gold will break through the $1,000-an-ounce mark it last hit in March of 2008, and not look back. There are credible people calling for $2,000-an-ounce bullion, and those who think the upside is even greater. Far greater. In this case, gold bought now could yield substantial capital gains when it is sold, and should be held like any other asset you think will appreciate. If that's the goal, a third to a half of your portfolio may not be outrageous, especially considering we've all been blindly keeping 80 percent of our net worth in one other physical asset we were convinced would rise forever—residential real estate.

On the downside, there are many clever people who, even in the months after the crash, think buying bullion is a dumb idea. For example Kiplinger.com columnist Bob Frick makes the point that gold has not performed well relative to stocks over the last seventy years (I agree with that), and a small holding will do little to improve your financial portfolio. As for gold soaring when world financial stress is rising, well, that has not actually happened either, he points out. Finally, "There's the scary reason to own gold: protection from a collapse of the financial system. If this happens, a single gold coin will be worth a wheelbarrow full of currency (think of Germany's Weimar Republic issuing 50-million-Mark bank notes in the 1920s). Unfortunately, we couldn't find any survivalists to interview for this story, but all the experts we contacted had a good laugh when asked about this scenario."

Well, "experts" also chortled and guffawed not so long ago when the alarm was raised that Canadian housing values were set to plunge, wiping out billions in equity. Where were all the "experts" when Wall Street masterminds were bundling together high-risk, default-prone mortgages, getting rating agencies to slap a Triple-A on them, and selling them to hedge funds who peddled to more smart bankers? How can any well-informed investor today not question institutional and conventional wisdom? What if we are actually on the verge of a new depression? While we wait for an "expert" to confirm it, the time to prepare would be long passed.

So how much gold should you have? As much as you want. In the happy event the world does not end, and we merely enter a new age of government-induced inflation, you can unload it for a profit.

IN WHAT FORM SHOULD YOU OWN GOLD?

You have several choices here:

- Gold coins—most typically Canadian Maple Leafs, American Eagles, or South African Krugerrands. Also popular are Chinese Pandas, English Sovereigns, Mexican 50 Peso 1947s, and the only euro bullion coin, the Austrian Vienna Philharmonica.
- Maple Leafs are an excellent choice, and are respected and accepted around the world. At .9999, it's also the purest gold coin on the planet and is available in various denominations, down to 1/20th of an ounce. There is no GST on Maple Leafs, but some provinces will nick you for sales tax on the purchase.
- Round bars and wafers—pocket-sized gold, available in quarter-ounce hunks up to one ounce.
- Bullion bars—typically sold by the ounce, in one, two, five, ten, 20, 100, or 400 bars, although the wealthy among us can also buy it by the kilo (1,000 ounces). These sell in general for a small premium over the spot price of gold, and that premium falls as the size of the bar increases. For example, the premium on a one-ounce wafer is typically $14, while that drops to $2 an ounce on a 100-oz slab. Buy one of 400 ounces, as my brother had me do, and there is no premium.
- Certificates—paper receipts for gold that you own but have not taken delivery of, kept on deposit by the dealer. These are usually available in minimum amounts of 10 ounces for gold or 500 ounces for silver. These are transferable (you can sell

them), are fully convertible into bullion, and do not attract sales tax, insurance fees, or fabrication costs.

- Gold company stocks—lots of those available on an exchange like the TSX, which generally (but not always) increase in value along with gold prices. Some of the better known companies include AngloGold, Gold Fields, Barrick, Kinross, GoldCorp, and Newmont Mining.

- Gold mutual funds—which invest in a basket of gold mining companies, or, as exchange-traded funds, mirror the precious metals index performance. Examples of the latter are iShares CDN Gold Sector Index Fund, iShares Comex Gold Trust, or Street Tracks Gold Trust.

WHERE TO BUY AND SELL GOLD

There are lots of precious metals dealers, and other places to get your hands on gold. You can find scores of them by doing an online search, and if you're buying authentic gold coins, like Maple Leafs, then go ahead and search for the best deal. Of course, be careful about payment and delivery—for obvious reasons. You can also order directly from the Royal Canadian Mint or, if you live in Ottawa or Winnipeg, drop in and buy your coins directly.

My favourite place to get any gold—coins or bullion—is Scotiabank. Together with its subsidiary ScotiaMocatto, this is the preeminent hangout for bullion addicts. They have tons of the stuff in their vaults buried deep under King Street in downtown Toronto, and the mechanism to sell you some through almost any bank branch in the country. Gold coins or bars can be delivered to your branch usually within a week or, if you go to a large centre (the best place is ScotiaPlaza at King and Bay), you can get them the same day.

HERE'S HOW TO BUY AND SELL IT:

1. At the bank branch you'll need a customer card and one piece of photo identification. If you are not a bank client,

then show up with two pieces of government-issued ID. If you come in to the bank to sell them some gold you already own, you'll also need to provide a social insurance number.

2. You can only use a set amount of cash to pay for gold: $3,000. (I guess this is to prevent guys from wandering in with boxes full of it and buying bullion for their brothers). The rest needs to go on a Visa card, or to be paid with a bank draft or certified cheque. You will have to stand there for a while the bank staff confirms the validity of the paper.

3. The bank will buy gold just as readily as it sells. To get the best price, ensure you bring in the original receipt of purchase.

The selling process can take a little time, since the bank may weigh the metal and confirm its purity before paying you. This step can be avoided if you have verifiable gold coins, or bullion with its receipt and certificate of authenticity. It sure helps if you have also left the coin, wafer or bar in the original plastic packaging.

If you're selling a gold certificate to the bank, or converting one into bullion, the signature on the paper must be guaranteed by an officer at the bank or trust where you are a regular customer. You'll be charged 0.025 percent of the value of the transaction, up to $5,000 US and half that on larger deals.

STOCKS: THE NEW WAY OUT, OR A WAY DOWN?

In the first week of November 2008, this letter arrived at my home:

Within the next ten days you will be receiving your month-end account statement. The month of October was one of the most difficult months that we have experienced in the financial markets and the account statements will reflect this volatility. Expecting a storm, I had positioned your portfolio conservatively. Because of this, it has weathered what turned out to be a category 5 hurricane relatively well. Your asset mix is defensive with lots of cash holdings and some high quality companies.

I take some comfort knowing that much of the down-turn we have seen was forced selling by speculators that had borrowed heavily to speculate in the markets. Once they have been washed out, the marketplace will abound with quality companies attractively priced. I know it may not be easy, but during times like this, it is more important than ever to stick to your long-term plan.

Obviously, that was from the guy who looks after my investment portfolio, and who has done that job since 1999. The letter was naturally a defensive move, but also good client management. As was intended, it made me brace for a shock. Two weeks later, here is what I discovered when my statements arrived:

Monthly market decline (DJII)	23.1 percent
My portfolio decline	4.57 percent

So, I had suffered an annualized loss of about 50 percent. I was happy! After all, the October massacre was only part of the story. As of mid-November, the market was down 46 percent from its peak, which meant it was the worst drubbing since the bear market of 1937-8, when investors received a 49 percent haircut. And this is why I have a portfolio manager, as should everyone who wants to expose their wealth to financial markets, especially now that we are in a period of wild volatility and irrationality. By the way, my portfolio is a discretionary one, which means my guy buys, sells, trades, and allocates as he sees fit, without my knowledge or trade-by-trade permission. I receive a monthly statement and a quarterly analysis and once a year indicate my risk tolerance which serves as a general guideline for his actions.

This was the breakdown of my main accounts at the end of October, 2008—the worst trading month since the crash of 1987 and, many believed, the primary mauling moment of a protracted bear market:

My accounts:

Canadian dollar account

	Fixed income	42.9 percent
	Preferred shares	2.49 percent
	Common shares	54.5 percent

US dollar account

	Fixed income	63.8 percent
	Common shares	22.3 percent

Retirement account

	Fixed income	99.5 percent

As you might imagine, I am asked all the time about the stock market, financial assets, personal investment strategies, and asset allocation. On a professional level, I live this stuff and follow the Dow, the TSX, the FTSE, Dax, Nikkei, and All-Ordinaries, often on an hourly basis, along with corporate earnings, market-making economic indicators, and my favourite crop of analysts. Especially now, how could you not be fascinated with this stuff? Never before has so much raw data been available to so many people in real time. Never in history has so much information been put in the hands of individual investors, along with the tools required to trade shoulder-by-shoulder with the professionals on trading floors or hunkered over terminals in the biggest brokerage houses.

It is incredibly empowering, and utterly dangerous. In fact, the greed-tinged buying and fear-induced selling of millions of small retail investors has helped increase market volatility and gore everybody's ox. In late 2008, for example, these investors sucked $175 billion out of the markets, half of that in the same month my holdings declined that four and a half per cent.

This was the first year in six that net equity flows had been negative, and it sure helped set a tone of retreat. Interestingly enough, there are some wise people who think the stock market—after the crash—was exactly where it ought to have been, even after a sickening 40 percent dive from 52-week highs. So, here are my rules of financial market investing:

STOCK MARKET ADVICE:
SURE YOU WANT TO DO THIS?

- After the crash, markets will be intensely volatile for at least a couple of years. Expect daily swings of hundreds of points. If you're already in the market, ignore them.
- If you are not invested in the stock market, and think it's a good time to jump in after the big decline, think again. It's not.
- As mentioned above, there's a large chance markets will rush higher, only to fall back into a deeper and more prolonged funk.
- Never, ever, ever borrow money to buy stocks. It's bad enough that you might have a mortgage, but with most loans made to buy stocks you will receive a "margin call" if the value of the security falls below the borrowed amount. Then you're forced to pony up the cash which often means a forced liquidation of the investment. That's exactly what happens in rapidly falling markets, bringing on news wave of selling.
- Don't buy individual stocks, since you just magnify your risk. Far better to invest through professionally managed mutual funds.
- If you insist on being a do-it-yourself investor, I'd suggest index funds, which match an overall stock indicator—whether it's the Dow, TSX, precious metals, emerging markets, or energy. Index funds are called "passive" which means nobody actually runs them—they just match what a segment of the market does. That also means they're cheaper to own than "actively" managed funds, with lower fees (called MERs—for management expense ratios). Another decent choice are exchange-traded funds (ETFs), which are essentially collections

of stocks and bonds that trade daily as do stocks, but offer low cost and tax efficiency. You can buy mutual funds from the banks, as well as from parent companies themselves, while ETFs are sold by the brokers.

- Expect a lot more crises between now and at least 2012. Markets almost always overreact to emerging events and perceived trends. For example, the dot-com mania brought a stock market binge, followed by a 90 percent collapse in the tech-heavy NASDAQ. The more recent credit binge saw a bulge in stocks values not matched by corporate earnings, and the trip back down was just as fast, with a 50 percent loss. Why would you want to be facing that on your own?

- As you can see from my own accounts, there is a big role for fixed income investments, especially for retirement funds you do not want to mess with. Also realize that bonds have an inverse relationship with interest rates, so when rates fall (deflationary times), bond returns go up. The opposite is generally true with equities, since corporations have better returns during years of inflation.

- Despite all you may hear and the macho bragging of your day-trading friends, being a buy-and-hold investor is actually the best strategy. Also pay more attention to companies which do business in a like manner to you—lots of cash on their balance sheets, and little debt.

- Never open an online trading account. Don't even think about it.

- Instead, determine your needs and hire the right person to meet them. If you want one individual to help you with RRSPs, an investment account, tax planning, and insurance, then latch on to a financial advisor, either a fee-for-service guy or one who is compensated by the companies whose products he or she buys for you. Over the last 15 years I've worked with literally hundreds of these people in communities across Canada and have seen firsthand the good they can do. If you trust your own judgment on real estate financing, insurance (except universal life—if you don't know what that is, ask an agent), RRSPs, and RRIFs, fine, but find a pro to do the market investing—common stocks, bonds, preferreds, and the like.

- If you have a security that's lost money in a general market downturn, you are best off to suck it up and do nothing. After all, there has to be a powerful reason to turn a paper loss into a real one, so if you don't need the money hang on and wait for what markets do in the long term, which is advance.
- If you can't stand a loss, even an unrealized one, then get out and never come back. Or, be like me—hire someone else to manage this stuff for you, and never think about except when you get an ugly letter.
- Never buy marketable securities with money you might need in a few years. This is called investing, not saving.
- And realize that being in the markets the wrong way could be a bad personal move. For example, my advisor picks individual stocks based on experience and research, which should mean making money in almost any environment. But if you loaded up on index funds, and the market eroded for a decade, you'd be devastated. Sound improbable? I'm sure it did to Japanese investors in 1990, shortly after the market had peaked at 39,000. But as deflation set in there (fuelled by a collapsing real estate bubble), the central government tried to resolve a banking crisis with a bailout program, and then crashed interest rates down to 0 percent. The actions ended up saving the country's financial system, but it also nuked the stock market, kept the economy in first gear, and decimated returns for stock market investors. The Nikkei, by the way, was solidly in the 8,000 range after the 2008 crash.

Hopefully that last point made you sit up a little. The comparison with Japan of almost twenty years ago is worth noting. The Japanese, too, had a real estate bubble and asset inflation which exploded when the average family could no longer afford the average home, and people working in downtown Tokyo were forced to live hours away from their jobs. Japanese banks were (of course) found to be sitting on massive loans based on hopelessly inflated land values, and the writing down of their assets caused a crisis. The feds rushed in with a rescue plan that pumped billions into the sector. And, to stimulate the economy, rekindle consumer spending and confidence, and try to inflate its way out of deflation, the central bank slashed interest rates until they were zero percent.

And it didn't work.

Flash forward to the US in current times, and you have almost the same scenario. A real estate-induced financial crisis and the resulting deflation threatens America and most of its trading partners. Governments in almost all Western countries, as well as China, are madly throwing money at the problem, while they slash interest rates to historically low levels. And as all this happens, the stock market flounders. Is there any reason to think the deal will work this time?

After all, this might be an even worse scenario than Japan faced. This time the real estate bubble was not just in a few big cities in one country, but in virtually every metropolitan area across the United States, as well as Britain, France, Spain, Iceland, Australia, New Zealand, Hong Kong, Sweden, Ireland, and Canada. This time, G-20 leaders convened in a first-ever emergency summit on the financial crisis in Washington, making it painfully obvious this thing was basically out of control. This time, central bankers burned up the phone lines coordinating interest rate cuts. And this time, an incomprehensible amount of money was transferred from governments (taxpayers) into the operations of banks and private companies.

This time, it was almost the perfect storm. Families saw the value of their principal asset, their home, plunge by as much as 40 percent, giving what economists call a "negative wealth effect." In other words, they felt trampled. This made people suddenly panic over mounting debts, since tapping into home equity was no longer an option, and they cut back on consumer spending. That accelerated a decline in economic activity, nailed retailers, car companies, and the construction sector, launching a tidal wave of layoffs. In short order, it was a vicious cycle eating away at consumer confidence. This was truly bad news in big developed economies where consumer spending and the service sectors are key drivers.

In other words, was this the start of a global deflationary death spiral? Would anybody dare invest in an environment like that? Is the stock market doomed?

Of course not. This is still the beating heart of capitalism. And while the global economy—and that of the US in particular—will have a terrible time in the next couple of years financing growing public debts and coping with millions of jobless people and retiring Baby Boomers, markets will not collapse. Not even when taxes rise (as they inevitably will), profits erode, and some major corporations fall by the wayside.

At some point, there will be a bottom. Society will level out after citizens have learned their lessons. Gone will be no-money-down real estate, home equity loans, and kids buying $70,000 SUVs. We will all become far more conservative—a trend which started almost immediately as the Dow was tumbling and the first new pink slips were being issued. As I mentioned, retail investors retreated from stocks and mutual funds with their tails between their legs, mortgage lending withered, and new car showrooms emptied. As usual, the pendulum swung from frothy, leveraged excess to Mennonite-style austerity and frugality. This neo-conservativism will lay the foundation for a market rebound, long before consumers realize the worst may have passed.

When that comes is an open guess. Maybe later in 2009. Maybe the next year. Or perhaps there will be another sucker bear rally which will eat what remains of your wealth. But at some point, a bottom will be seen, and then a rally. One reason to expect this is because too many governments have too much credibility at stake to let the rescue mission fail. World leaders are on the hook now, committed to intervention and cooperation. That means interest rates across the world will continue to drop, which always makes corporations happy and drives money into the markets. Another reason markets will rally is that good companies and quality stocks have been punished equally with the turkeys. Hard to see, long-term, how you can go wrong investing in energy, health care, information technology, or banking. Finally, once consumers stop feeling beat up and sorry for themselves, there will be a mess of pent-up demand which will send many share prices soaring. This is the direct result of government stimulus programs which halt the wave of home foreclosures and create hundreds of thousands of new jobs in infrastructure and other "New New Deal" programs. Barack Obama made history becoming the first black president. He has no intention of repeating history as the second Herbert Hoover.

So, here's my last rule of stock and mutual fund investing:

• Never try to time the market.

That means never panic and sell when markets drop, ensuring you lock in a loss. Equally, don't get greedy and rush to cash in when share prices are soaring. Simply remember the lessons we have all now learned (again) regarding real estate. When everyone wants it and prices are extreme, buying is fraught with risk because inevitably the market will correct, leaving you with more debt than equity. Conversely, when houses are unloved and prices have collapsed, there is far less risk in becoming an owner.

Normally the time between the first and last lows in a bear stock market is about eight months. But these are not normal times. Because we may have a serious touch of the Japanese disease the bear market could be extended for months, maybe years. So, if you have cash, there are probably better things you can do with it than buy stocks.

Ten low-risk things to do with your cash and tackle debt

1. Pay off high-rate credit card debt immediately.
2. Pay off car loans or student loans, even at preferred interest rates. Given the growing financial crisis and the threat of deflation expect a great number of these loans to be called without notice. Check your loan agreement—you may well be shocked at what you discover.
3. Make a pre-payment against the outstanding principal on your mortgage. This won't change your monthly payment, but it will shorten the amortization and decrease the amount of interest you fork over. Just $10,000 lopped off a $100,000 mortgage would shorten the repayment period by five years and save you almost $30,000. Now, that's a decent return on investment. (See more below)
4. Ensure you have a cash reserve able to pay family expenses for six months.
5. Buy some gold. Coins or bullion. Buy a safe.
6. If you do opt to stick the cash in a bank, remember the limits of deposit insurance: $100,000 per bank, per person. Another hundred grand with your spouse, if you like him or her enough.
7. Never keep money in a chequing account when you can flip it over into an account that at least pays some interest.
8. If you want a house, this is a far better time to buy one than any time in the last half-decade. Use that cash as a down payment after you haggle the best deal possible.
9. And if you still want to invest in the stock market, get a professional advisor and hand the money over.
10. Catch up on missed RRSP contributions, since you'll not only improve your future security, but get a big tax deduction by doing so. Stick that money in fixed-income securities, not a savings account.

A few weeks before the beginning of 2009, a few interesting things happened on the same day:

- Oil prices dropped to near $50 a barrel, a shocking collapse from $147 six months earlier. The government of Alberta responded by cutting its budget surplus forecast by 75 percent.
- Inflation in the US fell by the greatest amount in memory, eclipsing anything seen since government record started in 1947. Economists said they were shocked.
- GM Canada, teetering along with its parent on the edge of insolvency, revealed it was $4.5 billion behind on funding the benefits of its retired workers.
- New housing starts faded in the States to the lowest point since 1959, when data was first kept.
- The Toronto Real Estate Board revealed city housing sales were down 49 percent from year-earlier levels, prices were lower by 7.5 percent and listings had swollen by 37 percent.
- The owner of a solid brick, two-storey home in midtown Toronto dropped the asking price of his house once again, and threw in a new car—anything the buyer wanted—up to $15,000. But, there were no immediate offers. Said the agent, Michael Clarke, "It's a sign of the times."

Actually, it was a sign more of the times to come, than the times that were. And the sign says, "Warning."

If this book leaves you with a better understanding of one economic term, I hope it is deflation. Unknown in North America for eight decades, it now seems destined to shape the next few critical years, as we learn prices, wages, houses, cars, stocks, oil, and food can all spiral lower, propelling the value of money higher. In this environment, people with liquid wealth can snap up a nice house, a collectible auto, or shares in a great company for pennies on the dollar. But those with debts to pay on declining incomes get nailed.

Some mild deflation is not a bad thing since we can all do with cheaper groceries and more affordable real estate. But when deflation becomes entrenched, leading to corporate failures, lost jobs and a shrinking economy, it turns into something worse. The odds of that happening seem to grow with each passing day, suggesting that we all need to be cautious and—above all— struggle to get out of debt as soon as possible.

Some key actions I am urging you to take, by way of preparation.

TEN PLUS ACTIONS TO FIGHT DEFLATION

1. Understand that real estate is not a liquid investment. Buying in a rising market is a breeze compared with selling in a falling one. Because housing prices led us into non-stop inflation and historic levels of debt, it leads us now into deflation and owners' remorse. People with mortgages must use every tool at hand to reduce their exposure to debt. Those who are over-extended, facing an underfunded retirement, or who have unwisely put all their wealth in one place, must act.

2. Realize that your cash reserves are more precious than ever. If deflation takes hold, perhaps becoming depression, bringing the risk of social upheaval, cash is king since every day its purchasing power increases. That's why I have asked you to keep an emergency reserve, and why you must not exceed the limits of bank deposit insurance.

3. Hedge against potential problems with our national fiat currency, concerns about bank solvency, and global upheaval as economic woes spread with a position in gold. Wealth converted into bullion ceases to exist, is portable, and universally accepted, but must be aggressively protected.

4. Realize the opportunity posed by investing in assets such as

stocks and mutual funds since the financial markets will be the harbingers of renewed economic growth. After the crash of 2008, many of these assets lost more than half their value, and yet represented ownership of companies with strong balance sheets and large cash reserves. To position yourself for the inevitable recovery, you must be diversified with exposure to the market—but with a long-term perspective, and without the use of borrowed money.

5. Most importantly, kill debt. Take concrete steps to minimize the destructive impact of mortgage debt on personal finances. Go and see your bank now, today, to discuss these options.

6. Make any prepayment against the principal that your mortgage allows (as mentioned above); also, take out any new borrowing, or convert an existing fixed-rate mortgage when it comes up for renewal, to a variable rate loan. Interest rates have dropped dramatically, and will keep on falling as governments try to rescue economic growth. A VRM will save you money in this environment and, in fact, has proven over decades to be the cheapest way of borrowing mortgage funds. In a deflationary environment there is absolutely no reason to lock in and end up paying a premium rate to gain insurance against rate hikes which will not come.

7. When a loan comes up for renewal at a lower interest rate (and monthly payment) than in the past, shorten your amortization instead of opting for a lower monthly payment. That will pay the mortgage off faster and significantly decrease the amount of interest you have to cough up.

8. Increase monthly payments, if your mortgage allows that. Some will let you hike them by up to 15 percent, with that sum coming directly off the principal. Overall interest charges will drop and the loan will be retired years sooner. The best way of killing a home loan off is to switch from monthly to weekly payments. This can have the effect of dropping the repayment period by a decade or so, and can save you hundreds of thousands in interest on a sizable

mortgage. Simply take a usual monthly payment, divide it into four, and ask your bank to deduct that amount from your operating account every seven days, applying it to the mortgage (most easily arranged at renewal time, but no harm in asking for the payment frequency change to be made now). By doing this, you make the equivalent of one extra monthly payment per year, which does not sound like a lot, but the end result is impressive. You dramatically slow the accumulation of mortgage interest by chipping away at the loan principal every week, instead of every month, which increases equity and decreases debt. Do it.

9. Consider turning your own mortgage into a retirement fund, by setting up an RRSP mortgage. If you have cash or cashable investments inside your retirement plan, you can use those to replace all or part of an existing mortgage on your home. Now, instead of making interest and principal payments to a bank every month, you are making them into your own RRSP, which is a cool idea. You'll need the help of a financial advisor or a trust company to set this up, since the mortgage needs to be administered by a third party, and you have to charge yourself market interest rates. This is a somewhat complicated move, but completely worth the effort for many people who want better performance inside their RRSPs, without taking any significant risk to get it.

10 For cash-strapped retired people who want to tap into RRSP funds without being nailed for taxes, you can employ a strategy called the RRSP Meltdown which can be combined with getting money out of real estate and into your hands. This is also a tad complicated, and it requires the use of borrowed money (there are times when this makes sense). Take a secured loan against your home and invest the proceeds in financial assets, like dividend-paying stocks. The interest on that loan is deductible from your income tax. So, to make the interest payments, use funds withdrawn from your RRSP, which are taxable. That means your end tax liability is zero

and, in effect you have set up a non-registered investment portfolio financed by the government.

11. You can also combine some of these strategies to create a tax-deductible mortgage. For example, if you have a non-registered investment portfolio (outside of your RRSP) worth $100,000, and a $100,000 mortgage at the same time, simply cash in your investments and use the money to pay off the mortgage. Then take out a secured home equity for $100,000 and buy back those assets you previously had in your portfolio. Now all of the interest on your mortgage is tax-deductible, because the borrowing was made for investment purposes, giving you in effect a tax-deductible mortgage. This can increase your financial position greatly since instead of sending money off to the bank from your after-tax income, you get to subtract the loan payments from your taxable income. At the end of the process, you still have $100,000 worth of investments, and a $100,000 borrowing against your home, but your cash flow is much improved. A variation of this based on incremental investment loans is called the "Smith Manoeuvre," made popular by a BC financial author. Check it out, but be aware that its success rests on continuously rising financial markets, which you can no longer be assured of.

Cash, gold, stocks, mutual funds, bonds, investment loans, real estate, mortgages, RRSPs, and the use of tax laws and provisions—these are all some of the basic building blocks of a personal financial strategy, and yet most people today feel victimized by economic circumstances and are doing nothing. This is why you will see consumer confidence continue to scrape bottom for the next few years, with continuously lower prices for houses, disastrous retail sales, and a sharp increase in jobless numbers.

I cannot stress enough that times of rapid changes in the

economy, in the value of assets and in financial markets also bring unbridled opportunity. Once you have taken bold steps to eliminate debt, or make debt tax-deductible, to secure the liquid wealth you possess and to safeguard against a potential slip into depression, the way is clear to build new wealth. Even the grimmest of times will pass. There is no doubt whatsoever that inflation, rising prices, and ascending commodity values will return—thanks to the staggering buildup in government debt this crisis has engendered and the certainty of higher oil prices.

These are the days to be cautious and audacious at the same time. But first, you must determine in your own mind what lies ahead, and what actions you will take. The next chapter lays out options.

CHAPTER SIX

CHOICES

In volatile times there are ways to protect yourself, your family, and your wealth from threats. You can also prepare for the opportunities that always flow out of a crisis. In either case, you must take action.

As I write this book the economy's a mess, and there's no good reason to think things will get back to normal for a few years. In fact, "normal" is gone. We'll be paying the price for a long time yet for the stuff that happened between 2001 and 2008. We all borrowed far too much, fell for the myth of ever-rising real estate values, and failed to diversify, while governments worried more about playing politics than growing the economy or regulating bankers or lenders. There's a lot of blame to go around, without a doubt. But let's move on to what comes next, and what to do about it.

EXPECT THESE THINGS TO HAPPEN:

- Falling house values until at least 2010
- A large and growing federal budget deficit in Ottawa, starting in 2009
- Unemployment rising almost continuously for at least two years
- The banking and financial system rocked with bad assets and

a few failures
- Stunning stock losses before a market-led recovery starts
- Banks suspending dividend payments to stockholders
- Reduced exports and corporate failures as the US tries to protect jobs
- Fewer services as governments at all level struggle with a funding crisis

DON'T BE SURPRISED IF THESE THINGS HAPPEN:

- Neighbourhood food shortages as just-in-time delivery systems are disrupted
- Electricity brownouts starting as early as the summer of 2009
- A pension crisis as retirees find out about unfunded liabilities
- Real estate prices in Calgary, Edmonton, Fort Mac at 50 percent of 2006 levels
- A wave of mortgage defaults. Yes, in Canada.
- Scaling back of 2010 Olympics in Vancouver
- Bankruptcy of major Ontario homebuilders
- Martial law in some US and European cities to quell protests of unemployed
- Seasoned firewood climbing to $300 a face cord

HOPE THESE THINGS DON'T HAPPEN:

- Failure of a major Canadian bank, leading to emergency merger
- Canadian dollar falling with oil into 60-cent US range
- Banks ordered temporarily shut and restrictions on cash withdrawals
- Auto industry collapse, despite bailout. Ontario growing a rust belt
- Ottawa suspending social benefits. Pensions, child benefits etc., only for needy
- Cancellation of most credit cards, balances becoming demand loans

- Widespread shortages of food, gasoline, home heating fuels
- Mass migration from urban, suburban areas, especially in GTA, as people flee crime and seek self-sufficiency
- Economic activity falling by 10 percent, unemployment hitting 20 percent

While some of the above may sound extreme, enough will come to pass to make it clear we're in changed times. The decision each person must make is how to react, and to what degree. If you believe, for example, that the stock market will find a bottom, house prices will level off in a year or so, and Barack Obama will do whatever it takes to moderate a recession, then you may coast, doing little more than paying off some debt and hanging on to your job. On the other hand, if you see a new depression leading to social breakdown in a world without stable power, few debit or credit cards, food shortages, and no Internet, then all you care about is securing cash, gas, and shelter.

Between the extremes sit most of us, who want to look after our families and feel hopeful about next week. My conclusion for you: Doing nothing is no option.

Everyone by now should realize there's a new normal on the way. Young couples without any money won't be buying big new houses any more. Banks won't be selling toxic mortgages. Rating agencies will do their jobs properly. The government won't be lowering lending standards again. Big companies won't be so cavalier about loading up on debt. Fewer people will want to live in suburbia or ever buy an SUV. More folks will be worrying about falling prices than rising ones. Jobs will be harder to find, and pay less. Millions of retail investors will have lost all faith in the financial markets. You won't get any more credit cards in the mail. Saving will be in, borrowing out. Mortgages will be for paying off. Parking lots will sit where new condos were slated to rise. It will be much harder to borrow money. Energy conservation, self-reliance, and rugged individualism will be the new cool.

So, going forward, money will cost more and be harder to

borrow. The economy will ultimately stabilize, and then grow slowly as the banking system repairs. People will feel less wealthy and secure as they worry about their houses and jobs, which will hurt retail sales. Governments will be unable to cut taxes as their finances deteriorate with more demands and less revenue.

Families will be at the forefront of all this change. Thirty-year-old children will be moving back in with their parents. Baby Boomers will be most stressed just when they least want to be, selling the big house into a hostile market. Retired people will worry every day about their fixed incomes and pension security. University graduates will wonder how to pay off big loans on service sector salaries.

So, let's decide what the future will bring, in order to know what to do. Here are some likely options:

BEST-CASE SCENARIO

- Life returns to normal soon enough after brief recession
- Government bailouts work
- Stock markets bounce off lows, confidence is restored, investors pour in
- Banks stabilize, money flows again
- Real estate prices bottom out
- Governments end up with big deficits

PROBABLE SCENARIO

- Major recession takes hold, probably lasting years
- Significant companies disappear
- Unemployment increases steadily for two years
- Bear stock market continues
- Wealth evaporates as houses, financial assets decline in value
- Mild deflation grips the economy

POSSIBLE SCENARIO

- The financial system destabilizes from bad debt, hedge funds liquidate
- Some major banks go down, currency controls imposed
- Governments slash spending and services
- House values and share prices continue to dip to 1930s levels
- Daily life massively impacted as stores close, payments system fail

And of course:

WORST CASE SCENARIO

- Governments temporarily lose control
- Bonds fall into default, stock market trading periodically suspended
- No credit available, cash society develops, gold soars
- Millions of Boomers retiring into economic chaos
- Economy staggers through Japanese-style deflation lasting a decade or more
- University graduates have virtually no job prospects, Boomers fight to be Walmart greeters
- Stock market stagnates for years at 30 percent or less of former peak level, residential real estate never recovers to more than 40 percent of 2008 values
- Record government deficits add to ballooning public debt, guaranteeing big future tax increases and a crippled economy for decades
- Squatters move into abandoned suburban homes

WHAT ARE THE ODDS?

As US web economist Chris Martenson rightly asks in analyzing such scenarios, can you really put the odds of any one of them happening at 0 percent? I can't. Neither should you. There's a possible range of events, which goes from a minor disruption in your economic life (investments fall, real estate is hard to sell) to a major impact (job loss, wealth destruction) to all hell breaking loose (bank failures, depression, losing your home). This also means—if none of these things can be entirely ruled out—you have to take some action to mitigate against what you fear the most, or deem most likely. That action will depend on where you are today, how vulnerable you may be to coming events, and what's feasible for you to accomplish.

So, should a sensible, non-alarmist person worry about the "possible" or "worst-case" scenarios above? Or is this stuff too over the top? The answer lies in the nature of risk. If the possibility of something happening is not 0 percent, then a prudent person usually does something to protect against it. That's why I have life insurance, plus fire coverage on my house, and I'll bet you do too. We all understand the chance of our homes burning is negligible, but that if it did happen, and we weren't prepared, the outcome would be devastating.

That is exactly the case for action in contemplating a bank failure, the stock market losing 89 percent of its value or there being no functioning credit cards or ATMs, or food in Loblaws stores for a few months. If there's a greater than 0 percent chance of that occurring, then (like losing your home to a lightning strike or wild fire), you do something about it. You act. So why not act now?

Most people will put this off, hoping the problem just gets solved, that preparing is too much work or too unusual to contemplate, or it's far too overwhelming and extreme. After all, if you install a generator, plant a garden, set a safe into your basement floor, or quickly sell your home and move to the country, your kids and neighbours may think you're nuts. But chances are they have not spent ten minutes actually assessing the possibility of future events, taking stock of their own situation, or thought about the range of actions which would be sensible and reasonable. Like buying fire insurance.

Smart people identify risks and work to minimize them. So, if you believe (as I do) that there is at least a chance that over the coming years the financial system could break down, then you need to understand your vulnerability to this happening.

We've all become used to living in a society where just-in-time delivery stocks the grocery stores we depend on for food and the production lines of companies that supply us with products. Bank branches are now inoperable when they can no longer go online. Gasoline pumps and the furnace in your home won't work without electricity. People use debit cards to finance their daily lives, and have little if any cash. How much of a disruption would it take over the course of a few weeks or days to throw this society into chaos and confusion?

THIS IS NOT THE 1930s

Those who are convinced that we learned so much from the Great Depression that it can never be repeated may be absolutely right. But this is not the 1930s. We've surrendered our self-sufficiency to technology, with no paper money in our wallets and purses, no savings, no independent heat source in our homes, no corner greengrocer, no kerosene lamps, no well or water pumps, no vehicles we can repair, and little community support. How much of an event would it take to create a mess? Should we not be ready for a financial collapse or a breakdown in some of these gossamer systems?

IN DETERMINING IF YOU SHOULD CARE, ASK A FEW SIMPLE QUESTIONS:

- How little money would you need to get by?
- How long could you live on (a) your savings and (b) cash you actually have?
- What are your debts?
- How secure is your income? Could that change? Could you survive job loss? How long?
- How safe are your assets? Who controls them?

- How fast could you liquidate and access your wealth? Hours (bank cash), days (stocks, mutual funds, bonds) or many months (real estate)?
- If you woke up and heard on the news about a bank holiday that day, would you be okay?
- Do you know and trust your neighbours?
- Do you have a caring financial advisor?
- Do you have any backup systems at home (generator, wind-up radio, cellphone batteries, water, stored food, garden)?
- Do you know where all your energy comes from? Do you have backup?
- If the electrical grid went down, what would be your plan?
- Could you get around if the gas stations were not operating? How?
- Have you discussed any of this with your spouse or kids? Your next door neighbour?

If you can't respond to those questions with answers that give you confidence, then establish a plan that will provide you some. This doesn't mean you believe any kind of collapse is inevitable or imminent, only that it's possible and worth defending against.

Here's a concrete example: your bank closes for a while after the announcement that it suffered massive losses on credit default swaps suddenly provokes a run on deposits. Like the other Canadian banks, it is required by law to have only one dollar in its vault for every $10 it lends out. In other words, 90 percent of the people with money "in" that bank are out of luck if they all want it at once. Overnight, the bank asks the superintendent of financial institutions for permission to close in order to prevent insolvency. He grants it, of course.

DO YOU BELIEVE THIS POSSIBLE, YES OR NO?

- If the answer is yes (even if it's not probable) will you insure yourself against this likelihood, or not?

- If you take no action and the bank stays open every day going forward, your gamble paid off. You did nothing, and there was no consequence.
- If you prepare by having a six-month cash reserve in your home safe and the bank stays open, you can always put the money back in when things quiet down. You did something, and wasted a little time.
- If you prepare by having a cash reserve, and the bank fails or closes for a while, you have the resources to live normally while others about you panic and go without. You protected yourself.
- If you take no action and the bank closes, you're screwed.

That's how insurance works. If you believe you don't need any when it comes to our financial system, you haven't been paying attention. "A 1930s-style depression is not impossible by any means," wrote Stoneleigh, of The Automatic Earth, in an interesting post-crash piece on my blog.

We are still in the very early stages of the deleveraging process, where toxic "assets" are being shielded from the harsh light of day, so to speak. Eventually, there will be a mark-to-market event, however hard governments and central bankers try to avoid one, and that will precipitate a fire sale of assets at pennies on the dollar.

Such an event cannot be avoided, at least partially due to the creation of perverse incentives in the derivatives market. For instance, allowing a third party to take out a credit default swap against a company they do not own is analogous to allowing me to take out fire insurance on your home, thereby giving me an incentive to burn it down for profit. We have yet to see the "burning down for profit" phase, but it is coming, and when it does, the scale of counterparty risk in the CDS market will also be revealed. A large percentage of companies will not be able to collect on winning bets, and will therefore not be able to pay out on losing ones in turn. This will turn into a cascade event in a $62 trillion market, the effect of which will dwarf the credit destruction we've seen so far.

This event is truly global—thanks to the tight coupling in global financial markets, contagion inevitably spreads. The use of derivatives intended to mitigate risk has in fact led to systemic risk. There's a reason why Warren Buffet refers to derivatives as financial weapons of mass destruction.

If you follow the global media, rather than just the blinkered North American version, you will see how many countries are already teetering on the brink as a result of the credit crunch. Check out Iceland, or Pakistan, the Ukraine, Spain, the UK, Ireland, much of eastern Europe, and many more. Many of those countries had far worse housing bubbles than the US and have much further to fall as a result. To imagine Canada to be immune from such a conflagration is simply fanciful. Our real estate excesses have been less extreme, but our banking system is vulnerable, and our export economy will take an enormous hit.

This crisis is very much larger than merely real estate. Liquidity, the supply of which ultimately depends on trust, is the lubricant in the economic engine. Without a sufficient supply, that engine will seize up, just as it did in the 1930s. With no means to connect buyers and sellers, people can starve amid plenty, as they did then. In the 1930s both resources and real skills were plentiful, expectations were nowhere near so inflated and we had none of the structural dependencies on cheap energy and credit that we have now. Without cheap energy and cheap credit, our highly complex socioeconomic system cannot function. A long and painful readjustment is not just likely, but inevitable.

Talk of 1930s aside, the imminent threats are unemployment, wealth loss on the real estate and financial markets, corporate failures, and a tumbling net worth. If governments don't get it right—pouring billions into bailouts, crashing interest rates, intervening in financial markets—then things get more dire. It could be months after you read these words that we're still being shocked at the risks big financial institutions took, and the losing bets they made. And if Barack Obama disappoints a year or two into his term, another shining hope for corrective action will be gone. Once government has blown its wad, what silver bullet is left? This disappointment could be the driver of a new market decline in 2010, just when the US is dealing with the greatest budget deficit and accumulated debt in its history, while Ottawa walks into the deepest ocean of red ink in two decades. Why wait to find out what the impact will be on you?

Insurance today comes in many forms. Paying off credit card debt, setting up a weekly mortgage, buying a bunch of 50-litre gas cans at Canadian Tire and filling them, getting a hybrid bicycle, selling your house, installing compact fluorescent lightbulbs, or buying an index fund are all insurance. A major threat is losing wealth. A bigger threat is losing control. In a society where we have surrendered so much of our needs to others, it just makes sense to try and regain the upper hand. Even if the chance of a new depression is slim and economic recovery is upon us in a couple of years, how can you have gone wrong by getting your financial and personal life in order? You might waste some time and your spouse may make fun of you for having all the gas in the shed, but how bad is that? Compared to not being ready if cash or food became scarce, or to paying tens of thousands more in interest than you had to on your home loan, a little ridicule is the least of your worries. Especially since the last laugh will be yours.

THIS BRINGS US TO: *CHOICES*.
Life is full of them.

After the crash, the immediate future is uncertain and potentially full of risk. In fact this might be the situation we face for years and years. Looking at those who are losing wealth and hope as housing values plunge or the burden of debt mounts, it's easy to see how people get led into things by herd instinct. When magazines were full of articles on home decorating and luxury cars, when *Flip this House* was watched by millions, and curbsiding realtors orchestrated multiple bids on mediocre homes, it was easy to over-borrow and overspend and think it was okay because everyone was doing it.

The legacy now is too little saved, too much borrowed, and too many assets which are deflating. This is bad enough, but it could all get worse. Even if it doesn't, the crash and its aftermath have shown clearly that most of us need to pay way more attention to these choices.

Here are some things you can do, including some of the actions already listed in the pages of this book. I have divided them into three categories for those who (a) think this will all get better soon, but want more financial security; (b) believe the situation will likely get worse, and are determined to prepare; or (c) are convinced we're headed for a cliff, and refuse to go over.

Finally, I am often asked what my own prediction is for the years that lie ahead, and what measures I have taken to hedge against future events.

Since privacy equals security, and these are insecure times, you'll just have to guess at specifics. But starting in 2006 my goal was at pay down debt at all costs, simplify business entanglements, and cut exposure to things I could not control. Afterwards I substantially reduced my real estate footprint and secured property I felt offered me the greatest number of choices. Finally, I took steps to ensure that my family will always have functioning lights, a heat source, income stream, and resources in the event of the unknown.

Like you, I don't know what's coming. I'm not going to predict an apocalypse in order to sell books. I desperately want economic stability and prosperity for my neighbours and my country. I sincerely hope we are not entering the long, dark tunnel of deflation and despair that Japan was trapped in for 15 years or a rerun of the shorter, more brutal years of the Great Depression. I hope governments get it right. Get it fixed.

But I've also been in government, sat in Parliament, and seen things from that perspective. I've worked on Bay Street, know many of the players there, and how they operate. Like you, I'm part of the real economy, with money in the markets, wealth in real estate, and a functioning business with clients and employees. That last thing I want to see looming over my handlebars is the edge of that cliff.

So, many of the things on the lists that follow I have done, am doing, or will accomplish shortly. I've assessed the risks that might lie ahead, and determined the level of insurance that's reasonable. Hope you do the same. Let's compare notes, and keep this conversation going, at www.AfterTheCrash.ca.

LIST A: "WE'LL BE OKAY. TRUST ME."

The argument: *"History shows that most of the time economies grow and people prosper. Besides, we've learned so much about the 1930s and other downturns that no government is going to repeat those mistakes. We've got central banks, international cooperation, world trade, and an online global community tying everything together. This is a new age, and we're in control. So, we're correcting a little from a few overpriced houses and greedy investment bankers who are now fired. How bad can that get? I'll take measures to improve my finances, sure, but let's not turn into a bunch of survivalist nutbars here."*

1. Stay away from the real estate market. These are no days to sell because buyers are a bunch of greedy, selfish vultures.
2. Interest rates have fallen and bankers are hungry, so this is a good time to try and renegotiate your mortgage and get a better deal.
3. Arrange for weekly payments to replace monthly ones on your mortgage, which will cut down on the amortization period and save you a bundle on interest.
4. Write a family budget and try to pay off debt while still saving

10 percent of your income. You'll want the cash to buy up buckets of stock being dumped by suckers.

5. Get a financial advisor. Review your asset allocation.

6. Reassess your insurance. If you don't know about universal life, learn.

7. Don't sell stocks or mutual funds even if they have fallen in value and stayed there. Why turn a paper loss into a real one? Besides, selling is for weenies.

8. Downsize your Hummer to a Tahoe or Escalade.

9. Open one of those new after-tax savings accounts and stick in the maximum amount ($5,000) every year. You should do this in addition to making an RRSP contribution.

10. Buy or assemble a Bad Day Box. Just for ice storms, meteorites, and dump trucks backing into your house, though. No financial stuff.

LIST B: "SOMETHING'S GOING TO HAPPEN. I'M GETTING READY."

The argument: *"Sure I have faith in the system, but let's be realistic. The real estate market is falling, the stock market crashed, people have lost confidence and the government is throwing around billions, bailing out every failing business in sight. How can this just go back to being normal? Who's going to pay for all this? Everybody I know is worried about their job, nobody has savings, and mortgages sure aren't going down along with housing values. The US economy's in the soup and there is a recession around the world. I'm sure this is not the 1930s all over again, but some days I really worry where we're headed."*

1. Plant a backyard vegetable garden. Replace those useless mulberry and birch trees and cedars with apple and peach trees.

2. Don't buy a new vehicle from a car company, or a dealership that may not be in business next year. When you do buy, be obsessed with fuel economy but don't pay a big premium for a hybrid. Soon they'll all be hybrids—cheaper ones.

3. Have most of your family net worth in one place, like your

house? Bad idea. Work towards diversifying, to make sure you have a mix of real assets and financial ones. Once it looks like the economy might improve, stock markets will rebound far faster and earlier than real estate.

4. Install a generator at home or at the cottage or out-of-town property, or both. Don't cheap out with a garage special but instead go for a permanent installation complete with electric or automatic start, transfer switch, and separate panel box. Natural gas or gasoline-powered, depending on your assessment of fuel avails during a disruption.

5. Don't have an out-of-town property? Get one, cheap.

6. Have a credit card-freedom day once a week, and use cash.

7. Never buy a house so costly or with such a small down payment that monthly mortgage payments consume more than a third of your gross income.

8. Pay down debt. List every single debt you have, with interest rates and payments, and then attack those which are most costly (credit cards usually top the list). Never ever use plastic to pay the outstanding minimal balance on another card.

9. While you're at it, create a list or database of all your assets. This will remind you of where your money went, and also gives a snapshot of things you might be able to dispose of to raise cash in difficult times. Also think hard about the liquidity of what you've got. Some things, like real estate, can be dogs to get rid of, while mutual funds can be sold in hours. Art and antiques in tough times are worth a fraction of their value in a robust economy.

10. If you lose your job, don't be proud. File for unemployment benefits—the sooner you do it the faster you'll get some cash.

11. Learn how to make preserves from your garden and fruit trees (relishes, pickles, jams).

12. When it comes to selling real estate, don't be a Fizzbo (FSBO—for sale by owner). Never try to sell your house in a declining or soft market by yourself, without a realtor or getting on MLS. You will simply never get the wide exposure you

need to maximize the price or even find a greater fool.

13. Get a realtor who has experience in the area—not just with getting a lot of listings, but getting a lot of sales. Always ask for a marketing plan and comparables.

14. Ask a realistic amount for your house. Get it wrong, and you could wait a year for an offer.

15. You never get a second chance at first impressions with your home, and in this market impressions matter. Work on curb appeal (gardens, walkways) and remember the best investment you can make is paint.

16. Save your money through an automatic monthly deduction like a payroll savings plan for CSBs or for the purchase of mutual fund units.

17. By investing in funds on a weekly or monthly basis you will even out the swings of the marketplace. Impress your mother-in-law by telling her you dollar-cost average.

18. Get a credit card that doesn't charge an annual fee.

19 Imagine that you lost your job, and live like it. Chop unnecessary expenses, don't buy stuff you don't need, and budget.

20. Maintain a cash reserve—enough to pay your household expenses for a minimum of three months and, better, six months.

21. Regarding that cash, best to keep it in smaller denominations—tens and twenties—if you think you might need this to make purchases in disruptive times. Chances are it will be very hard for most vendors to make change, so small bills are best.

22. If you're taking out cash because of insecurity about your bank, or the viability of federal CDIC bank account insurance, then go for large bills—hundreds (note than only banks will now accept thousands).

How to build a Bad Day Box

Every home should have a Bad Day Box in this age when a power failure alone can render most of our daily support systems useless. It takes just a few hours and a few hundred dollars to put together the things that can make the difference between misery and want and relative comfort (you can assemble one yourself or order it online from sites such as xurbia.ca). This is not guns-and-ammo survivalist material but rather common sense. Put these items in a waterproof container like a clear plastic storage unit (Canadian Tire or Home Depot), or a wheeled garbage pail with a lockable top. Make sure everybody in your household knows where this is.

In addition, ensure you have lots of bottled water and canned foods in your kitchen, in a stash that you rotate every six months. You need to maintain one gallon of water per day per person, for at least three days.

The box should include (modified from lists found at www.72hours.org, plus www.getprepared.gc.ca, the federal government web site):

- Manual can opener and other cooking supplies
- Paper or plastic plates, and utensils
- First Aid kit and instructions
- Wind-up radio (mine is AM/FM/SW with built-in siren, flashlight, and reading lights)
- A copy of important documents and phone numbers
- Warm clothes and rain gear
- Heavy work gloves
- Disposable camera
- Cellphone and spare battery
- Unscented liquid household bleach and an eyedropper for water purification
- Personal hygiene items including toilet paper, feminine supplies, hand sanitizer, and soap
- Plastic sheeting, duct tape, and utility knife for covering broken windows. You can never have too much duct tape.

- Tools such as a crowbar, hammer and nails, staple gun, adjustable wrench, and bungee cords.
- Blanket or sleeping bag. I prefer thermal blankets, which weigh next to nothing.
- Large heavy duty plastic bags and a plastic bucket for waste and sanitation
- Any special-needs items for children, seniors, or people with disabilities. Don't forget water and supplies for your pets, and medical prescriptions.
- Camp or barn-type "hurricane" lanterns, plus at least two gallons of kerosene
- Matches—several boxes of them, plus waterproof container.
- Books to read
- Cash

23. With emergency cash, be very careful when you make your withdrawal. Call ahead to inform the bank and give them time to get it together in the denominations you wish. Have them count it away from the wicket on the automated counting machine, and take a secure lockable briefcase or shoulder bag (strapped across your body) to transport the bills.

24. Don't tell anyone other than your spouse about the cash, or the Bad Day Box, for that matter.

25. If you have multiple credit cards, pay off all but one, seal the others in an envelope, and put them in the safe.

26. Buy a little extra at the grocery store each week—like canned goods and paper products. If the power goes out, none of these can be purchased at stores which rely on bar code readers and electronic cash registers.

27. Regarding a home safe, remember that the most secure possible device is one the thieves can't find.

28. The worst safe is a free-standing one, no matter if it weighs 800 pounds and is impenetrable. If there's a burglary, you won't see it again.

29. Get a safe with both a lock and a combination wheel or an electronic keypad, as well as concealed hinges and live-locking bolts. Install it out of sight in a wall, in a cold air return, or defiantly cemented into your basement floor.

30. The safe is for cash, of course, but also for precious metals, passports, credit cards, wills, insurance, and things that can be used in an identity theft.

31. If you're taking out a mortgage, get a variable rate one. Interest rates are going to be ultra-low for a few years, and there is absolutely no need to pay more for a fixed term as insurance against future rate increases. Won't happen.

32. Never panic after watching CNN money reporters, and sell your investments at a loss.

33. Come to an agreement as a family on finances and budgets. Kids should know times are volatile and they might not get what they want. Ditto your spouse. Remember what the exasperated Wall Streeter said at the height of the crash, "This is worse than divorce. I've lost half my net worth and still have my wife."

34. Consolidate your loans. Consider a personal loan or secured line of credit at a low rate to wipe out high-rate credit card debt, for example, then have regular payments taken from your account.

35. If you are one of the millions who do end up losing their employment in this storm, try to be cool and composed. Ask about parting benefits and severance package, and getting a letter of credit. Don't sign anything in the initial meeting, but be as professional as possible, since you do not want to burn any bridges.

36. Don't be loath to try and negotiate your severance. If you're being offered employment counselling and you don't want it, try to trade that for another week of pay or extended dental benefits, for example.

37. Don't waste money having a lawyer chase your employer with a weak wrongful dismissal action. Most go nowhere. By the

same token, if you are laying someone off or terminating them, make sure you respect their rights, know your legal obligationand give the required notice or payment in lieu of.

38. Practice losing your job. Imagine what you'd say, or what you'd do the next day. If it happens, it will not reflect on you, but on your employer's failure. It's okay. You'll see.

39. Live on one salary. Bank the other.

40. Skip the vacation this year. Only if you work underground in a Cape Breton coal mine can you justify spending a few thousand precious recessionary dollars on two weeks of sand and surf, sipping gin from a hollowed-out coconut served by a topless mermaid. We miners know.

41. Consider banking with a credit union. These outfits often offer lower fees on financial products and services, along with reduced loan rates and easier access to mortgage funds.

42. Be on guard against credit card fraud as the economy heads south. Never let someone swipe your card twice without giving you a transaction cancelled receipt for the first one. This is how card skimming takes place.

43. When using an ATM, be aware of who is around you when withdrawing money, and ensure they do not see your PIN being entered. Hang on to the banking machine receipts.

44. Online credit card use has exploded, but so has fraud. If you're going to order online, pick reputable merchants and sites with full security (look for the padlock symbol). Never send credit card numbers and expiry dates in emails. Don't give out the info on the phone. Check your monthly statements. Be on the lookout for negative option billing, like domain name registration renewal fees which are processed without your approval.

45. Use debit, not credit.

46. If you're spending more than 10 percent of your net take-home pay on credit card or consumer loan debt, you're paying too much. Fix that.

47. Back to real estate. Buy houses with a future, sell ones without

a hope. Well-located and affordable urban condos or bungalows will retain value, and "green" houses will be the most
desirable as energy-induced inflation replaces this fear-
induced deflation. Unloved will be leaky, 1980s-era
four-bedroom houses, and the suburbs in general. Small town
and exurban properties are hot.

48. Use the Internet as a tool for buying and selling real estate.
Online research can give you an excellent snapshot of relative
property values (www.mls.ca rules), while establishing a website for your own sale can help generate leads.

49. Thinking of buying distressed US properties at bargain-basement prices from dumb Americans? Go ahead. They're
waiting for you, sucker.

50. If you sell a home, give serious consideration to renting rather
than buying. This can reduce your cost of living while shield-
ing you from a still-falling market. Do the math, and realize
that home ownership is a losing financial proposition unless
you can be sure capital gains from price appreciation will over-
come cost.

51. If you do rent, check out overstocked markets like Toronto,
where thousands of condo units are on the market owned by
reluctant landlords who wished they were flippers. Don't like
the asking rent? Offer what you want, plus free months, free
parking, free health club, free decorating.

52. If you're buying a house, it should never cost more than four
times your annual income

53. If the average family of peers living in your area cannot afford
the home you are considering buying, don't buy it.

54. Get a part-time job. Obviously this will give you more money
to help pay off debt or amass savings, but it will also open a
second window in the case of job loss. In that instance, the
psychological benefit alone is worth it.

55. Find a financial advisor, because the last person you want
managing your money is a total amateur who's learning on
the job (get a mirror). A fee-for-service planner will analyze

your life and give you a plan. A planner who is compensated by the companies whose products he or she buys for you (mutual funds, insurance, etc.) can also be an immense help. I have a guy who just manages my investment account, and charges me a percentage of its annual value.

56. Use online banking? Change your password monthly.

57. If you know what you're doing, get a home equity loan. This is secured by the money in your real estate, comes at a bargain interest rate, and the interest is deductible from your income taxes if the loan is used to buy income-producing or capital gains-producing assets (rental real estate, stocks, mutual funds etc.). But understand that unlike unsecured borrowing (credit card debt, for example), this is a loan that can be called and if you can't pay, you could lose your home.

58. For that reason, sophisticated investors are far better off arranging leverage through a financial advisor who can get you an unsecured investment loan.

59. Catch up on missed RRSP contributions. You are allowed to go back and accumulate all those payments you never made, and stick them in your retirement plan, netting you a big tax refund. If you don't have the money, borrow it and use the refund to repay the loan.

60. If you lose your job, you can withdraw money from your RRSP to live on, but make sure you keep the amounts to less than $5,000. That will minimize the withholding tax the bank takes off.

61. Start paying more attention to your credit score. Don't ignore bills you dispute or let card balances run past 50 percent of your credit limit. Pay bills off promptly (online is best). Download your credit rating and address any problems or mistakes.

62. If you are shopping for a mortgage, shop around. The best deal is not necessarily going to come from your usual bank. Pay attention to repayment privileges and get a home loan that lets you increase monthly payments, make lump sum

payments, or change the payment frequency (for example, to weekly).

63. Get a mortgage with insurance against job loss. For example, some Canadian credit unions offer coverage giving up to $2,500 a month for nine months in the event you are laid off.

64. Negotiate a lower credit card fee. Often just by calling the card issuer and asking for a better deal, you can receive one, lowering the annual percentage rate by up to 6 percent.

65. Don't take a cash advance on a credit card. That's what ATMs are for. Banks, too.

66. Back to real estate. If you bought a home in the last few years with little, or nothing down, be very aware of falling into negative equity. That's when the market value of your home dips below the amount you owe on the mortgage. In that situation, you'd be seriously underwater when selling, since your proceeds would be reduced by a realtor's commission. If you just walk, you'd still be on the hook for the full mortgage amount, plus legal costs, even if the property went under power of sale and yielded less. One option: Approach the lender for more favourable mortgage terms.

67. If you can't stand the thought of your home devaluing, then get serious about selling. There is a high degree of probability that real estate values will continue to fall into 2010, and may not stabilize for some time after that.

68. Pay down debt before you save money. Always.

69. Realize your savings account is paying you about 2 percent. Your credit card balance is costing you between 11 percent and 19 percent.

70. Do not procrastinate. Do not be seduced by a few days of rising stock markets. Don't wait until the grocery shelves are emptying and they're lined up 40 deep at Canadian Tire. The time to prepare is immediately after reading this page. Go.

PLANNING AHEAD: GO-BAGS

A Go-bag is an essential companion to your Bad Day Box. In a flood or a fire, you'd have to bail out, so why not get ready in advance? Put this stuff in a backpack and prepare one Go-bag for each family member and make sure each has an ID tag. You may not be at home when an emergency strikes so keep some additional supplies in your car and at work, considering what you would need for your immediate safety.

- Flashlight, preferably wind-up
- Radio—battery operated or wind-up
- Batteries
- Whistle
- Dust mask
- Pocket knife
- Emergency cash in small denominations and quarters for phone calls
- Sturdy shoes, a change of clothes, and a warm hat
- Local map
- Some water and food
- Permanent marker, paper, and tape
- Photos of family members and pets for re-identification purposes
- List of emergency point-of-contact phone numbers
- List of allergies to any drug (especially antibiotics) or food
- Copy of health insurance and identification cards
- Extra prescription eyeglasses, hearing aids, or other vital personal items
- Prescription meds and first aid supplies
- Toothbrush and toothpaste
- Extra keys to your house and vehicle

LIST C: "THIS WILL GET BAD. I'M OUTTA HERE."

The argument: *"This is a watershed moment. How can it not be? Wall Street investment banks collapsed, the real estate market collapsed, the stock market collapsed, the car business collapsed, commodity prices collapsed, governments panicked, jobs vanished, and people are too freaked out to spend. Savings are nil and debt has never been higher. We're paying the price for two decades of excess, insane borrowing and over-consumption. And this will get fixed in a couple of years? I don't think so. We're on the edge of global financial, economic, infrastructure and social breakdown, in which everything could dive in a few days. If you are not spending every hour getting ready for what's obviously coming, well, good luck."*

1. Assess where you live. There is a high degree of likelihood you will need to worry about food production, energy, and personal security. None of these things will be possible in most urban locations.
2. Expect basic government services to break down, or be drastically scaled back as provinces and especially local governments run into a financial crisis. Transportation services will be the first to go—no 24-hour subway service or weekend buses, then no public transit at all, as available resources are put into policing. But it will be insufficient to maintain order.
3. Stockpile water, and more water, along with purifiers and filters. Bleach should also be held in reserve for emergency purification. Plastic bottles of all sizes will be in high demand.
4. Cherish self-sufficiency. The wealthiest citizens will be those who have an independent water supply, a septic system, a heat source (such as a pellet stove), and enough land for a garden and animal husbandry.
5. Get out of the suburbs. Fuel shortages and lack of policing will make life there miserable.
6. Get a generator. Now. Natural gas-powered units such as the Generac Guardian will provide reasonable security in an urban setting as almost all the infrastructure is buried.

Propane is not a good option, since delivery requires reliance on trucks which need diesel and electric pumps. Gasoline-powered units are a good choice, so long as you take immediate measures to stockpile fuel.

7. Wire the generator properly through a transfer switch and pre-select the circuits you will need to power, segregating them into a new panel box.

8. Secure the generator, since there is a 100 percent chance someone will try to steal it. Never leave a portable generator in your garage. Wherever possible, attempt to conceal your installation.

8. Install a woodstove or an airtight insert capable of burning wood, coal, or pellets. Do not attempt to do this in a new home designed for a low-heat gas fireplace, since you will need to erect insulated stovepipe. Don't expect a fire truck in eight minutes after you dial 911 anymore.

10. Get a supply of seasoned hardwood—at least two years' worth. Do this now, because the price of a cord will at least triple by next winter. Do not store this outside in a visible location.

11. Stockpile those things which you will not be able to buy—aluminum foil, toilet paper, paper towels, soap, shampoo, baby supplies, garbage bags, paper plates, plastic cups, and utensils.

12. Get a bicycle for each person in your household. This is essential since even if you can find gasoline, it will expensive. Outfit the bikes with baskets or carriers front and rear (lightweight saddlebags are excellent). Get an air pump and tire repair kits. For longer trips consider an electric hybrid bike, which has a range of approximately 30 km.

13. Buy a bunch of books and board games.

14. Get out of your mortgage. Sell your home if it is not ideally suited for self-sufficiency, and do it now, regardless of what kind of monetary loss you experience. The last thing you want is an unrepayable debt on a useless house.

15. Then buy a big, used RV and park it on a cheap acreage two hours out of town.

16. Always have a first-aid kit handy—in the vehicle, at home, with the bicycle. Emergency rooms will be jammed, and there are many medical issues you can treat effectively yourself. To help, get a practical up-to-date medical dictionary and guide.

17. Get a year's worth of prescription meds now.

18. Having a functioning radio is far more critical than a television since that will be medium of choice for emergency government messages. Buy two or three now that run on batteries, or can be charged by winding-up. Get ones with lights and alarms built in. Needless to say, stockpile batteries and keep them in a dry place where they will not freeze.

19. Get cash. Install a safe. Wear a concealed moneybelt.

20. What's left of your liquid wealth after you obtain enough cash for two years of expenses should be converted into gold bullion. Either recognized coins such as Maple Leafs or one-ounce bullion bars clearly marked by the assayer and showing purity.

21. Always keep your gas tank full.

22. Get a barbecue. Have at least two full propane tanks at all times, plus a ready supply of charcoal and lighter fluid. Get a BBQ with a side grill designed for boiling water or keeping meals warm.

23. Backup your computer onto CDs and put them in your safe.

24. In tough times, low-tech is often the best tech. Go to Canadian Tire, TSC, or a country hardware store and buy kerosene-fuelled hurricane, or barn, lanterns. They are cheap, will hold a flame in almost any weather, are portable when lit and throw out vastly more light than a candle. Kerosene is also very cheap, at least for now.

25. Make sure you get a small pump and funnel to fuel the lamps from the kerosene containers. The cost will be less than $5, but this is essential gear.

(Most items available online at www.xurbia.ca.)

Caring for the animals

Keep a collar, current licence, and up-to date ID tags on your pet at all times. Consider having your pet microchipped.
Make sure your pet is comfortable being in a crate, box, cage, or carrier for transport.

Keep an updated list of trusted neighbours who could assist your animals in case of an emergency

Remember that animals react differently under stress. Keep dogs securely leashed and transport cats in carriers or pillowcases.

If your pet is lost, contact the nearest animal shelter to report your pet missing. When it is safe, return to your neighborhood to search and distribute "Lost Pet" posters; include a current picture of your pet.

Make a Go-bag for each pet. Include:

- Sturdy leashes and pet carriers. A pillowcase is a good option for transporting cats and other small animals. Muzzles for dogs. Food, potable water, and medicine for at least one week
- Non-spill bowls, manual can opener and plastic lid
- Plastic bags, litter box and litter
- Recent photo of each pet
- Names and phone numbers of your emergency contact, emergency veterinary hospitals and animal shelters
- Copy of your pet's vaccination history and any medical problems
- Portable fencing or baby gates

If you must leave your pets behind:

- Inform animal rescue workers of your pets' status: On your front door or in a highly visible window, use chalk, paint or marker to write the number and types of pets in your residence. Include their location in your home and the date that you evacuated.

- Leave plenty of water in a large, open container that cannot be tipped over.
- Leave plenty of food in timed feeders to prevent your pet from overeating.
- Do not tie up your pet in your home.

26. Ensure you own, or have access to, basic tools. Include plastic sheeting and duct tape, plus a bow wood saw, hatchet, axe, and gardening tools.
27. Get basic fishing tackle.
28. Keep several clean, new garbage pails with lockable lids and wheels. They are ideal for transport of large quantities of water, for storage, or to move firewood.
29. Get several seasons' worth of vegetable seeds and put them in your safe.
30. Plan to have two methods of communicating with family and others, such as email, cellphones or two-way radios.
31. Buy a fold-up, portable solar panel capable of charging a cell phone or car battery.
32. Learn to preserve the bounty of your garden and fruit trees through canning and preserving. Learn how to avoid contamination.
33. Maintain a supply of food in your home capable of providing basic nourishment for at least three months. Canned vegetables, tuna (in oil), powdered milk, KD, rice, beans, honey and sugar, vegetable oil, canned fruits, stews, tea bags, soups, peanut butter, nuts, raisins, and cereals, for example. Don't forget to keep a manual can opener and vitamins with these things, and an ample supply of bottled water.
34. Buy two wind-up flashlights and enough folding thermal blankets for each member of your household.

35. Put $100 into rolls of quarters and keep them for emergency phone calls. Make sure you know the location of payphones near your home.
36. Keep a large quantity of energy snacks and nuts in your emergency area, and packed into individual go-bags.
37. Install a clothesline and buy pegs.
38. Keep emergency supplies in your vehicle, including water, a blanket, extra clothing, first aid kit, shovel, candle in a deep can, matches, wind-up flashlight and maps. In the trunk, salt or sand, jumper cables, windshield fluid, flares and chain.
39. Your car trunk is a valuable steel storage cabinet. Consider keeping tools and other essential supplies there.
40. Consider a weapon. If you go this route, it will take time to apply and qualify for a Firearms Acquisition Permit, and then there are strict rules governing what you can own, where you can use it and how you must store it. Consider joining a shooting club so that experienced gun owners can assist you.
41. A better idea is to build a network of community support. If the financial crisis ends up crippling governments' ability to help citizens, then they will have to help each other. Consider a community garden, a neighbourhood security watch and patrol, or co-generation of power, and put together a list of skills your neighbours possess so you know who to ask for electrical, plumbing or appliance repairs. Board up and secure abandoned homes in your area, tow off derelict or suspicious vehicles, and consider road barricades, but only after social order has broken down.

AFTER THE CRASH

Are some of the above suggestions extreme? Most people will readily answer that they are. Some will not. Some folks will wonder how any of this factors into a financial book. Others will quickly see the connection in a time when our collective pursuit of consumerism and comfort has led into debt and danger. We've surrendered a great deal of control over our lives, to banks, governments, utilities, and institutions we cannot influence or access.

After the crash we know much more about the fragility of our system and how it broke down.

We hope for better days. But hope is not action. That's for you. Take care.

HOW TO CONTACT THE AUTHOR

ON THE WEB

Garth Turner invites you to be a part of an ongoing discussion arising out of this book, and his companion book on the troubled future of real estate, *Greater Fool*. Garth's daily blog on the economy, investments, personal finance, real estate and the turbulent times we are in is constantly updated, and fully open for your comments and questions.

Access this valuable resource through either of these web site addresses:

www.garth.ca
www.AfterTheCrash.ca

THROUGH EMAIL

To send a comment directly to Garth Turner, use this email address. It will reach him immediately.

garth@garth.ca

IN PERSON

Garth Turner is one of the country's most experienced, exciting and motivating public speakers. He has entertained and educated audiences across North America, and will consider a live appearance for keynote addresses, public or private seminars, client workshops, industry or consumer shows, conventions or community groups. Contact him directly by phone or email:

(416) 346-0086
garth@garth.ca